Danny Akin (Ph.D.) currently serves as the President of Southeastern Baptist Theological Seminary and is a Professor of Preaching and Theology.

Richard Caldwell (D.Min.) is the Pastor-Teacher of Founders Baptist Church in Spring, Texas. He is also the campus pastor of The Expositors Seminary.

H.B. Charles, Jr. is the Pastor-Teacher of Shiloh Metropolitan Baptist Church of Jacksonville and Orange Park, Florida. In 2017, he was elected President of the Southern Baptist Convention Pastors' Conference.

Christian George (Ph.D.) is the curator of the Spurgeon Library and Associate Professor of Historical Theology at Midwestern Baptist Theological Seminary.

Jim Hamilton (Ph.D.) is Professor of Biblical Theology at The Southern Baptist Theological Seminary, where he has served since 2008. He is also Pastor of Preaching at Kenwood Baptist Church.

Carl Hargrove (D.Min.) is a staff pastor at Grace Community Church in Sun Valley, California, and is the Dean of Students and Associate Professor of Pastoral Ministries at The Master's Seminary.

Juan Sanchez (Ph.D.) is Senior Pastor of High Pointe Baptist Church in Austin, Texas and Assistant Professor of Christian Theology at The Southern Baptist Theological Seminary.

Owen Strachan (Ph.D.) is Associate Professor of Christian Theology at Midwestern Baptist Theological Seminary in Kansas City, Missouri.

A BIBLICAL
ANSWER FOR
RACIAL
UNITY

KRESS
BIBLICAL
RESOURCES

Kress Biblical Resources
The Woodlands, Texas
www.kressbiblical.com

ISBN: 978-1-934952-33-7

Printed in the United States of America.

CONTENTS

PREFACE

This book has been compiled from messages originally given in January 2017 at the Truth in Love conference, hosted by Founders Baptist Church in Spring, Texas. Each chapter is based on the corresponding sermon transcript from that conference.

Since this work is a compilation of nine biblical expositions and one biographical survey, it is not intended to be an exhaustive treatment of the Bible's teaching on racial unity. Neither should one expect every possible application or nuance of the issue to be dealt with. It does, however, offer biblical insight into the core elements of the Scripture's answer for racial reconciliation and unity within the church—and in our world.

It is our prayer that it will help bring biblical clarity to our age that is so filled with confusion on this matter—and ultimately, glory to our great God and Savior, Jesus Christ. To him belong eternal praises, from a people united by the gospel of grace and the Spirit of God.

ONE

THE SUFFICIENT WORD ON RACIAL UNITY

Richard Caldwell Jr.

Therefore, having this ministry by the mercy of God, we do not lose heart. But we have renounced disgraceful, underhanded ways. We refuse to practice cunning or to tamper with God's word, but by the open statement of the truth we would commend ourselves to everyone's conscience in the sight of God. And even if our gospel is veiled, it is veiled to those who are perishing. In their case the god of this world has blinded the minds of the unbelievers, to keep them from seeing the light of the gospel of the glory of Christ, who is the image of God. For what we proclaim is not ourselves, but Jesus Christ as Lord, with ourselves as your servants for Jesus' sake. For God, who said, "Let light shine out of darkness," has shone in our hearts to give the light of the knowledge of the glory of God in the face of Jesus Christ. (2 Corinthians 4:1–6)

C. S. Lewis wrote: "I believe in Christianity as I believe that the sun has risen; not only because I see it, but because by it I see everything else." I think it's the last part of that statement that may be the most profound. "I believe in Christianity as I believe that the sun has risen; not only because

I see it, but *because by it I see everything else.*" As believers, we see everything else by the light of Christian truth—by the light of Christ. That's what we *should* be able to say, but is that really true of us?

A World in Chaos

We live in a chaotic world. We see the chaos all around us all the time. It's on our television sets as the news tells us what's going on in this city or that city, this march, that march. At times, we know it in a very personal way as well.

The chaos is explained by sin. And sin's chaos is manifested in every realm of life. Man knows a personal chaos because of sin. When you think about some of the things that we deal with in our world—gender confusion, homosexuality, personal sin on all sorts of levels—they all are examples of sin's confusion in man's own person.

We know confusion and chaos in our closest relationships. This world is full of broken homes and broken lives. We know sin's confusion in our societies and communities. We live in a world at war with itself, because it is a world steeped in sin and idolatry.

When men do not find their hearts satisfied by God, their hearts will not be satisfied. James addresses this in his letter: "What causes quarrels and what causes fights among you? Is it not this, that your passions are at war within you? You desire and do not have, so you murder. You covet and cannot obtain, so you fight and quarrel. You do not have, because you do not ask" (James 4:1–2).

Those verses expose what is often true of us. We're not looking to the Lord for the satisfaction of our hearts. And even when we do ask, we often ask with wrong motives. "You ask and do not receive, because you ask wrongly, to spend it on your passions" (James 4:3).

This is the chaos that sin produces in a life that has self at the center, pride on the throne, selfishness at the core. All of this chaos manifests death. Sin made its entrance into the world, and death came as a result. Adam and Eve ate of the tree of the knowledge of good and evil and they died, just as the Lord had warned. God told the truth. Now every person born into the world is born spiritually dead, and exists in a state of spiritual darkness.

And so, we recognize that we live in a world full of people who are full of evil desires, which emerge from evil hearts—haters of God, and haters of men. As the book of Jeremiah describes it, the hearts of men are deceitful above all things and desperately wicked (see Jeremiah 17:9).

Our world is at war with itself because the natural man, the unregenerate man, knows nothing of the love of God. The person without Christ is incapable of loving God, and therefore incapable of really loving people. We too, before coming to Christ, lived in this state of war and death. Titus 3:3 says, "For we ourselves were once foolish, disobedient, led astray, slaves to various passions and pleasures, passing our days in malice and envy, hated by others and hating one another." That's the world we live in. That's the world of lost humanity.

There is no political fix for what ails this world. There is no human solution to the problem. There is no cultural analysis or commentary or social program that can fix what's wrong.

An Answer for the Chaos

There's only one answer for such a world, there's only one hope in the midst of the chaos, and his name is Jesus.

When the light of the gospel confronts the darkness, when the clarity of the gospel cuts through all the confusing voices that we hear in this world, then the sovereign Spirit of God unshackles our souls. When God says, "Let there be light," and the light of God shines into the darkened soul of man so that Christ is seen on the pages of Scripture in all of his beauty—and he is loved and he is believed in and embraced for life—there's a new order, a new creation. Old things pass away, all things become new.

Through that saving work, peace replaces chaos, love replaces warring, compassion replaces pride, God brings order out of disorder. All these new creations, one soul at a time, form one new man in Jesus Christ. Christ is at the head of a new humanity, a redeemed human race.

The Word of God Is Sufficient

This is why we preach the Word of God. To state it simply, we believe in the sufficiency of Scripture. It doesn't matter what the problem is. It doesn't matter what controversy you want to discuss. It doesn't matter what issue we want to organize around, and meet around, and think about. The Word of God is sufficient to address the issue. Are you convinced of that?

We must be convinced that we don't need any more cultural commentators—we have enough. We don't need virtue posturing or virtue signaling: "Oh, let me let everybody know how culturally sensitive I am, so they'll all think better of me."

We don't need a Christian version of the world's song. We desperately need to know what the Scripture says. Is there a place in this world where we can find the truth? The church must be the one place on the planet where people can find the truth.

In 1 Timothy 3:15, the apostle Paul says, "If I delay, you may know how one ought to behave in the household of God,"—the family of God— "which is the church of the living God, a pillar and buttress of the truth."

In 2 Corinthians 4:1–6, Paul addresses the issue of truth in a chaos-filled, death-ruled world. He's facing attacks from false teachers that have influenced the Corinthian church. So, he's facing attacks from unbelievers, but he's also facing attacks from immature believers who have been influenced by the false teachers.

He's been forced to defend himself. He finds no pleasure in this, but he has to do it for the sake of the gospel, and for the sake of the church. In chapter 3, he began to lay out some characteristics of a God-approved workman, someone who is equipped by God's grace to shepherd the people of God. And at the end of that section, he wrote about the message of God's workman. A truly approved servant of God is known not just by his character and not just by his manner, but also by his message. A truly approved servant of God is known by what he preaches.

The God-approved workman, a preacher of the new covenant, preaches the gospel and declares the glory of Christ. Preaching the truth brings its own kind of conflict. Paul is in the midst of that kind of conflict, but he will not be ashamed or dissuaded. He will preach the Word of God, and he will preach the Word of God in the way that it ought to be preached.

In 2 Corinthians 4:1–6 we can see five truths that reveal how the Word of God should be declared in a world like ours.

1. God's Word is to be preached with constancy: "Therefore, having this ministry by the mercy of God," he says, "we do not lose heart" (2 Corinthians 4:1). Lose heart—*egkakeo*—in this context speaks of both becoming discouraged and fearful.

In the midst of preaching and meeting with the resistance, it's possible to become discouraged. Nobody likes conflict and rejection.

And out of fear of meeting with that kind of rejection and conflict, God's people are tempted to tame down the message of God's Word. Paul says, "I won't do that." We don't do that. We do not lose heart. Our preaching must be faithful—enduring, consistent, and unchanging.

Paul has known new-covenant mercy, God's mercy, in his own life. He has known God's mercy in his own conversion. He has known God's mercy in his calling.

This is a man who persecuted the church, who was formerly a blasphemer. Now the Lord has not only saved him but also given him the unimaginable privilege to declare that gospel of grace in Christ, his Savior. He is a living exhibit of what he preaches.

Knowing God's mercy as he does, how can he play the coward? He does not shrink back from the truth of the gospel. He will not allow what is wicked, what is evil, what is bad to move him away from the declaration of God's Word. Neither can we. In the face of wicked hostilities on display in our world in so many different ways, when sensitivities run so high, and it feels dangerous to simply say what God has said in his Word—*we have to be convinced we can't do better than that*. We can't do better than to simply, faithfully, courageously give the answers that Scripture gives. Preach the Word of God with constancy and courage.

2. God's Word is to be preached honestly: "But we have renounced disgraceful, underhanded ways. We refuse to practice cunning or to tamper with God's word, but by the open statement of the truth we would commend ourselves to everyone's conscience in the sight of God" (2 Corinthians 4:2).

Transparency, purity, and sincerity characterize faithful gospel ministry. In verse 2 Paul says, "We refuse," meaning to disown or renounce. He renounced, first, the hidden things of shame. The ESV reads, "But we have renounced disgraceful, underhanded ways," or more literally, "the hidden things of shame." Paul was not going to be involved with anything that he would have to hide because he would be ashamed of it.

Second, he mentions "craftiness," or in the ESV, "cunning." The term is recorded five times in the New Testament. It is never used in the positive sense. It refers to being capable of anything. It came to mean trickery, craftiness, cunning. Someone has referred to it as the art of misrepresentation.

This is what characterizes Satan. As Paul indicates in 2 Corinthians 11:3, "But I am afraid that as the serpent deceived Eve by his cunning, your thoughts will be led astray from a sincere and pure devotion to Christ."

Paul would not be engaged in some secret life of sin, or in things he would have to be ashamed of. He would not try to be a salesman, learning the art of winning people over in a way that's not honest, pure, and sincere. He would not be characterized by distortion or corrupting of the Word of God. The word translated "tamper" is sometimes used of corrupting gold or wine with inferior ingredients. Paul would not add anything that would corrupt the message.

So, viewed from the standpoint of the preacher—free from shame. From the standpoint of the presentation—free from craftiness. From the standpoint of the message—pure, not calculated to snare by adding one's own ingredients. That's the honesty of preaching. But honesty in preaching is not just avoiding those things. It's also a positive commitment to something more.

Second Corinthians 4:2 reads, "But by the open statement of the truth we would commend ourselves to everyone's conscience in the sight of God." Paul's preaching was characterized by openness and clearness. The root of the Greek word for "open statement" has in it the image of a light or a lamp. False teachers are engaged in secret lives of shame; Paul turned the light on.

He turned the light on by declaring the Word of God. Preachers need to stop trying to be profound. Rather we need to be clear and recognize what is truly profound in preaching. What is profound is not our thinking about the Bible. What is profound are not our individual opinions formed from our reading of the Bible. What is profound is the *Bible*. Preach the Word.

Those who do preach the Scriptures are appealing to the consciences of men: "but by the open statement of the truth we would commend ourselves to everyone's conscience." We must not try to persuade people by making them think well of us. We must aim at the consciences of people with the truth of God's Word.

It is "by the open statement of the truth" that we "commend ourselves" to their consciences. When God's servants simply, sincerely, and consistently set forth his Word, their genuineness is demonstrated. That has an effect in the consciences of people.

Charles Hodge said this: "Those ministers who are humble and sincere, who are not wise in their own eyes, but simply declare the truth as God has revealed it, commending themselves to people's consciences; that is, they secure even the testimony of the conscience of wicked people in their favor."[1]

And notice that all of this is before the face of God. The end of verse 2 reads: "in the sight of God." With integrity before God.

3. God's Word is to be preached perceptively: Preach the Word of God with *courage*. Preach the Word of God with *honesty*. Preach the Word of God *perceptively*. Notice 2 Corinthians 4:3–4: "And even if our gospel is veiled, it is veiled to those who are perishing. In their case the god of this world has blinded the minds of the unbelievers, to keep them from seeing the light of the gospel of the glory of Christ, who is the image of God." We must perceive that preaching is a revealing work. Where the Word of God is being preached, God's sovereign work in souls is being revealed.

In chapter 3, Paul wrote about a veil over the hearts of people, over the minds of people. When Moses is read, they cannot understand. Why? There's a veil there.

In verse 3 Paul says, "if our gospel is veiled, it's veiled only to those who are perishing." As we preach the Word of God, we need to know in advance that not everybody is going to be able to see it. To some, the

---

1   Charles Hodge, *2 Corinthians*, ed. Alister McGrath, Crossway Classic Commentaries (Wheaton, IL: Crossway, 1995), 71.

message we preach will be an aroma of death leading to death. To others, it will be an aroma of life leading to life (see 2 Corinthians 2:15).

The Scriptures clearly confirm that men are culpable for their own sin. And just as clearly, they confirm that where people are brought to saving faith and their lives are transformed, all glory belongs to Jesus Christ, for that's the sovereign work of God. Thus, we're able to simply set forth the Word of God without the burden of salesmanship or human manipulation.

People are already blind due to the fall. Dead, blind, enslaved, unable to please God—this is what the Bible says so clearly. But realize that Satan has an ongoing mission of blinding people. He is at work in this domain of darkness pandering to people's fallen desires, affirming them, confirming them, baiting them, leading them all the way to their damnation, confirming who they are by nature in this fallen world.

Satan opposes the clear, unmixed, unashamed declaration of the glory of Jesus Christ. Thus, preaching must promote the clear, unmixed, unashamed gospel of the glory of Jesus Christ.

4. God's Word is to be preached selflessly: Next, in 2 Corinthians 4:5 Paul says, "For what we proclaim is not ourselves, but Jesus Christ as Lord, with ourselves as your servants for Jesus' sake."

We come as stewards of a message. We are simply servants of Jesus Christ. That is, we are to preach in such a way that we make clear the message is not *us* and the message is not from *us*. It's not *our* wisdom. It's not *our* answers that people need. They need *Christ*. They need *his* truth. *Christ* is true wisdom for men.

We are not the message. Christ is the message. How do you make sure you don't preach yourself? You preach the Word of God—the Bible.

5. God's Word is to be preached hopefully: Finally, 2 Corinthians 4:6 tells us God's Word is to be preached *hopefully*. "For God, who said, 'Let light shine out of darkness,' has shone in our hearts to give the light of the knowledge of the glory of God in the face of Jesus Christ."

Creation illustrates the power of God in the new creation. There you were, there I was, in our darkness, in our bondage, in our blindness, and someone preached the gospel. And God said, "Let there be light," and there was light. And now from the pages of God's Word we are able to see God's glory in the face of his Son. We see Jesus for who he really is. We see that the eternal Son of God left heaven and came to earth and took to himself a sinless human nature, and lived a sinless life under the law on this earth. And then he died on the cross as a substitute for sinners and was raised from the dead bodily, and has ascended into heaven. He's coming again. Jesus is able to save the uttermost, anybody who comes to him by faith.

That message was preached and God opened our hearts just like he did for Lydia in Acts 16:14, so that we paid attention to the things we were hearing. And God granted us repentance and faith in Jesus. Though we've never seen him with our physical eyes, we loved him. And we turned from our sins and we trusted in him for life. That's how we came to Jesus. That's the hope for sinners.

Salvation is a sovereign work. It is a creative work. God calls into being what was not there before. It is an effectual work. He secures that which he seeks. And it's a transferring work. He takes these people out of one domain, and he places them into the kingdom of his dear Son (Colossians 1:13).

We're not dealing with a superficial problem. We're here in a world of chaos. And the reason why it's so chaotic is because of sin and because of death and because of darkness. And it's of a nature that *we* can't fix.

We must realize from the outset that what this world most desperately needs is for the church to be the church—the pillar and support of the truth. The world must be able to find the truth on display in the church. For this to happen, we must preach the Word of God with constancy, honestly, perceptively, selflessly, and hopefully. We need to apply the gospel truths of Jesus Christ to every situation—including issues of cultural and racial reconciliation.

Orthodoxy is not enough. We must also have orthopraxy. We must take the truth of the gospel and apply it to this situation.

TWO

THE BIBLICAL STRATEGY FOR RACIAL UNITY

H. B. Charles Jr.

Now in these days when the disciples were increasing in number, a complaint by the Hellenists arose against the Hebrews because their widows were being neglected in the daily distribution. And the twelve summoned the full number of the disciples and said, "It is not right that we should give up preaching the word of God to serve tables. Therefore, brothers, pick out from among you seven men of good repute, full of the Spirit and of wisdom, whom we will appoint to this duty. But we will devote ourselves to prayer and to the ministry of the word." And what they said pleased the whole gathering, and they chose Stephen, a man full of faith and of the Holy Spirit, and Philip, and Prochorus, and Nicanor, and Timon, and Parmenas, and Nicolaus, a proselyte of Antioch. These they set before the apostles, and they prayed and laid their hands on them.

And the word of God continued to increase, and the number of the disciples multiplied greatly in Jerusalem, and a great many of the priests became obedient to the faith. (Acts 6:1–7)

One day, a disgruntled reader wrote the editor of his local newspaper, complaining that the paper was not what it used to be. The editor replied, "It never was." The same could be said about the church. But this does not stop us from looking back for some non-existent "golden age" of the church.

The mistake is understandable. As we look around us at the contemporary church, it seems the word of God is rejected, the name of Christ is reproached, and the work of the Spirit is quenched. The proper response is to look forward and put our hope in the imminent day when the Lord Jesus will glorify the church and present her to himself without spot or blemish. But because we can only see through a glass darkly, it is hard for us to wrap our minds around what the church will be. So we look back and put our hope in the empty possibility of becoming what we used to be. But the church has never been what it used to be. The Acts of the Apostles makes this clear with no room for any reasonable doubt.

There is a real sense in which the church was at its best at its birth. But as you read Acts, you will find that the early church experienced many of the same growing pains the church faces today, including racial reconciliation.

At the birth of the church on the day of Pentecost, people from around the world heard the gospel and trusted the Lord Jesus Christ for salvation. Acts 2:4 reports: "And they devoted themselves to the apostles' teaching and the fellowship, to the breaking of bread and the prayers." Christian fellowship around gospel truth continued and grew in subsequent chapters, even in the face of religious persecution. But in Acts 6, the unity of the church suffers its first direct attack. Racial disharmony was the means of attack. Acts 6:1 reads: "Now in those days when the disciples were increasing in number, a complaint by the Hellenists arose against the Hebrews because their widows were being neglected in the daily distribution."

The passage begins by telling us when these events took place. It was during a time when the disciples were increasing in number. This was a strategic attack on the growing church. As people were hearing, believing, and obeying the gospel, a complaint rooted in racial animosity arose. This was no Jew-Gentile issue. Hellenists—Greek-speaking Jewish

Christians—complained against the Hebrews—Aramaic-speaking Jewish Christians—because their widows were being neglected during the daily distribution of food. In a real sense, this problem was more cultural than racial. After all, the people involved had more in common than the things that separated them. Ultimately, the complaint that arose was a spiritual matter. And the twelve apostles led the church to address the racial tension spiritually.

This is how we should work through the growing pains of racial reconciliation today. The church cannot adequately address racial issues by trying to be something it is not. The church must be the church. The church must keep the main thing the main thing. The church overcomes racial tensions by maintaining spiritual priorities.

The Challenge of Racial Unity

Every church has its problems. Do not be fooled by "the church of the Immaculate Perception." There are no perfect churches—not your church, not the church down the street, not that church on television that you watch. Here are two facts about any church you enter: nothing is as bad as it seems, and nothing is as good as it seems. Every church has problems. Even the early church had its shares of problems. The opening verses of Acts 6 tell us about two problems the early church faced.

Verse 1 reveals a problem: "Now in these days when the disciples were increasing in number, a complaint by the Hellenists arose against the Hebrews because their widows were being neglected in the daily distribution." The bad problem of dissension arose because of the good problem of growth. Acts 2:37 reports that 3,000 souls were added to the church on the day of Pentecost. Acts 2:47 reports that the Lord was adding to the church daily those who were being saved. By Acts 4:4, the number of believers had grown to about 5,000. Acts 6:1 reports that the disciples were increasing in number. What a great problem to have! Souls were being saved, disciples were growing, and lives were being changed. The enemy must have been angry about this, so he attacked the church.

The church had been under direct attack. In chapter 4, the church faced severe persecution. But after Peter and John were arrested, censured, arrested, and beaten, the church praised the greatness of God and prayed for greater boldness to proclaim Christ. In chapter 5, the church faced moral corruption, when Ananias and Sapphira lied about the money they received for selling their property. But God quickly judged them, causing them to drop dead in the assembly. And the holiness of the church was preserved. But there was still another way to undermine the early church: internal dissension. This is what we find in chapter 6.

For the record, this was not tension at the church potluck. This was a big issue. In the early days of the church, many Jews lost their homes, jobs, and families when they trusted Christ. Especially vulnerable were widows, who did not have government agencies, special grants, or insurance policies to take care of them. The burden of caring for widows rested squarely on the shoulders of the church—rightfully so. And the church took these matters seriously.

Acts 2:44-45 reports: "And all who believed were together and had all things in common. And they were selling their possessions and belongings and distributing the proceeds to all, as any had need." Acts 4:34-35 reports: "There was not a needy person among them, for as many as were owners of lands or houses sold them and brought the proceeds of what was sold and laid it at the apostles' feet, and it was distributed to each as any had need."

The church was pulling together to make sure there were no unmet needs among them. By Acts 6, the church had a great supply of financial resources to minister to the needs of the saints. And I am sure many widows were being helped. But for whatever reason, the Hellenistic widows felt overlooked in the distribution. There is no hint in the text that this was something intentional. Yet the Hellenistic widows complained. If this matter had not been addressed immediately, it could have become a means of division, disunity, and disharmony among the saints.

Verse 2 reports the apostles' response to the problem: "And the twelve summoned the full number of the disciples and said, 'It is not right that we should give up preaching the word of God to serve tables.'" Commentators read the problem of dissension as an issue of racial or economic division. But the response of the twelve—the original eleven apostles and Matthias—tells us that this dissension was actually a spiritual problem. In the face of racial, cultural, and ethnic discord, the response of the apostles was first and foremost pastoral.

There are two vital issues at stake: Preaching the word and serving tables. Both matters were legitimate and significant. The apostles had enough discernment to recognize that one of these important issues had become a problem that could potentially hinder them from focusing on the other important issue. The dissension among the saints arose to distract them from the scriptures. Satan used division at the table to hinder the declaration of the truth.

The twelve's response to this distraction is stated in clear and direct terms: "It is not right...." Notice how they spoke of this issue in moral, ethical, and spiritual terms: "It is not right that we should give up preaching the word of God to serve tables." The twelve were not saying that they were above waiting tables or that this kind of practical service was beneath them. Rather, they were speaking as men who knew, embraced, and refused to compromise what the Lord had called them to do. As the spiritual leaders of the church, it was their God-given responsibility to proclaim, explain, and defend the word of God and the testimony of Jesus Christ.

In fact, the ministry of the apostles was so intimately connected with the ministry of teaching and preaching that Acts 2:42 calls the message of Christ "the apostles' doctrine." The apostles knew that the health and growth of the church depended on the faithful preaching of God's word. So, they would not neglect the vital work that the Lord had called them to do, to do the important but secondary work that others could do. They refused to be distracted from the scriptures.

And I think this is the challenge for us—to keep the main thing the main thing. Paul's charge to Timothy is the Lord's charge to the church:

> I charge you in the presence of God and of Christ Jesus, who is to judge the living and the dead, and by his appearing and his kingdom: preach the word; be ready in season and out of season; reprove, rebuke, and exhort, with complete patience and teaching. For the time is coming when people will not endure sound teaching, but having itching ears they will accumulate for themselves teachers to suit their own passions, and will turn away from listening to the truth and wander off into myths. As

for you, always be sober-minded, endure suffering, do the work of an evangelist, fulfill your ministry. (2 Timothy 4:1-5)

The first church I served was in Los Angeles. At the age of seventeen, I was called to succeed my father, who had led the church for forty years. It was the church I grew up in. I knew everyone. Everyone knew me. All of my family was in this church. In 2008, I moved to Jacksonville, Florida, to a new congregation. I did not know anyone in the city, much less the church. As we were preparing to make the transition, I talked to a friend of mine who had gone through a couple of pastoral transitions over the years. I asked him, "What do you think I should focus on when I get boots on the ground in Jacksonville?"

He responded by telling me a parable. These bandits descended on a town to rob the bank. As they scoped it out, the locals had the bank guarded extremely well. They'd never be able to break in. But they didn't give up. The bandits regrouped and came up with an ingenious plan. They went out into the fields and began to set the barns on fire. The locals and all the authorities and officials ran out to help put the fires out in the barns. While the locals were putting the fires out in the barns, the bandits robbed the bank. My friend was saying to me, "Whatever you do, guard the bank."

Friends, I would challenge us that the matter of racial reconciliation is the same way. We must guard the bank. We must make sure the main thing is the main thing. The challenge for predominantly black churches in the United States is to make sure we do not transform the church into some civil rights organization where the gospel is lost.

Anybody, any group, can put new clothes on a man. Only the gospel can put a new man in clothes. As important as these matters are, we must make sure we keep the main thing the main thing—the gospel of grace and forgiveness through Jesus Christ, the authority of the Word of God, and the call for humble obedience—even in the face of ethnic and cultural differences and problems.

The Strategy for Racial Unity

In Acts 6:3–4, Luke records the apostles' strategic response: "Therefore, brothers, pick out from among you seven men of good repute, full of the

Spirit and of wisdom, whom we will appoint to this duty. But we will devote ourselves to prayer and to the ministry of the word."

There was tension arising because the Hellenists were being neglected in the daily distribution, so the twelve called the entire congregation together. The apostles planted a flag, determined to maintain their spiritual priorities. But they did not dismiss the real issues involved. They proposed a strategy to address the problems. There are a lot of lessons to be learned from verses 3–4, but may I suggest we focus on what they teach us about Christian servanthood. This is a strategy in which the leaders and the members are organized to minister to one another in Christlike servanthood. Christlike servanthood is the strategy for racial unity.

In Philippians 2:1–5, Paul reminds us that there can be no spiritual unity unless there is true humility. We are to do nothing through any selfish ambition or conceit, but with lowliness of mind or humility we're to honor others as better than ourselves. And each of us is to look not after our own interests only, but also after the interest of others. We are to have the mind of the Lord Jesus Christ.

I remember in the church I served in Los Angeles, out of nowhere, these white kids started showing up for service. They were not connected to anyone in the church. And they did not hang around after the service for us to meet them. They would just show up and then leave. We later discovered that these were young people from an InterVarsity group at the University of Southern California. A couple of the girls somehow learned about the church and visited. Because they were influential in the group, the rest of the kids followed them to our church. On Sunday morning, they would just pile into the church and at the end of the service make their way out.

But one of them, a young man named Philip, hung around one day and asked for a meeting. I agreed, of course, but did so nervously. I was, in my mind, sure he was going to come into that meeting to tell me everything he did not like about the church, namely, that we were probably too loud. On the day of the meeting, Philip, a Hispanic brother, walked into my office, and we got the chance to know each other. I'd never had a meeting like this before, and I haven't had too many like it since. When I finally kind of pushed him down to business and asked, "How can I help you?"

he said, "I only came with one question. How can I pray for you?" I just dared to take him up on it and told him how he could pray for me. And he had one more request: "Do you mind if I periodically check in and just see the status of these things that I'm going to regularly be praying about for you?"

We became friends. We became partners in the gospel. We became fellow elders in that church. And in the last service I was able to lead— the final weekend of my tenure at that church—it was that brother who stood on behalf of the entire elder board to announce a blessing on me and my family.

Just through that simple act of coming in and offering to serve me, in that little way, more conversations began, and more relationships developed, and more walls began to break down. Not by protests and arguments. Rather, by service.

We see in Acts 6 the apostles' strategy of Christlike servanthood. Notice the service of the membership, verse 3: "Therefore, brothers, pick out from among you seven men of good repute, full of the Spirit and of wisdom, whom we will appoint to this duty."

John MacArthur comments here:

> Biblical church organizations always respond to needs and to what the Spirit is already doing. To organize a program and then expect the Holy Spirit to get involved in it is to put the cart before the horse. We dare not try to force the Spirit to fit our mold. Organization is never an end of itself but only a means to facilitate what the Lord is doing in His church.[2]

The apostles did not volunteer, and refused to be drafted into serving tables. They instead proposed a strategy to have the members minister to one another. This apostolic strategy is the biblical standard of the New Testament church. Ephesians 4:11-12 says, "And he gave the apostles, the prophets, the evangelists, the shepherds and teachers, to equip the saints for the work of ministry, for building up the body of Christ." The ministry

---

2   John MacArthur, *Acts 1–12*, MacArthur New Testament Commentary (Chicago: Moody Press, 1996), 176-177.

of the pastor-teachers is to equip the saints for ministry. This requires that the saints do their part to free up the pastors to focus on equipping. It also requires that pastors be humble enough to get out of the way and allow the saints the freedom to minister to one another.

Notice, as the apostles sent the membership out to seek those who would carry out this task, *they emphasized godliness, not giftedness.* One of the mistakes we make in church is to promote people for the wrong reasons. We promote people who are highly gifted. We promote people who have strong personalities. We promote people who have been members for a long time. We promote people who have a lot of money. We promote people who are successful in the business world. Churches promote these people, even though they have no clear evidence of spiritual maturity. In so doing, we doom the church to spiritual immaturity, because the members become what the leaders are. This is how ministries in the church or congregations themselves become hostages to carnal-minded people. It is because we have not kept our priorities straight.

The bottom-line is that if you want a godly church, promote godly people. Verse 3 says: "Therefore, brothers, pick out from among you seven men of good repute, full of the Spirit and of wisdom, whom we will appoint to this duty." The church was to select men who had a good reputation throughout the congregation. This was a high standard, considering the church had over 5,000 members at the time.

Likewise, they were to select men who were filled with the Holy Spirit. This qualification did not mean the chosen men had to have some supernatural endowment. According to Ephesians 5:18, it is God's will every Christian be filled with the Spirit. They were not to select men who were worldly, carnal, of self-willed. They were to select men who obviously submitted to the leadership of the Spirit. Furthermore, they were to choose men who had wisdom. Godly leadership is needed to help the church keep its focus on the things that matter the most.

Jesus faced two great crisis moments during his earthly ministry—one at the beginning of his ministry; the other at the end. The first is recorded in Matthew 4:1-11, where Jesus was tempted by the devil in the wilderness after fasting for forty days. The later crisis is recorded in Matthew 26:36-46, in the Garden of Gethsemane. From these two episodes, Jesus gives us tools to help us to do the Lord's will when a crisis arises: scripture and prayer. The apostles must have learned this lesson from the teachings and example of Jesus. In verse 4, the twelve state their ministry priorities: "But we will devote ourselves to prayer and the ministry of the word."

These are the essential tools of Christian ministry: prayer and the ministry of the word. I made this statement in one setting, and someone asked, "What's more important, prayer or the ministry of the Word?" I answered that question with a question. "If you are thirty thousand feet in the sky on a plane, which wing is more important, the left wing or the right wing?" If either one malfunctions, you are going down." I am not diminishing conversations, activities, and works that help bring us together. But the plane is going down if the church does not keep as its priority prayer and the ministry of the Word.

The apostles were men of prayer. They viewed it to be their divine duty to pray. It was not what they did as they led the church. It is one of the essential parts of their leadership. They had no dichotomy that separated work and prayer. Prayer was their work! This is what the church needs today. We need spiritual leaders who are men of prayer. Spiritual leaders must be devoted to private prayer.

Our private lives should be characterized by communion with God in prayer. A prayerless Christian is an oxymoron, a contradiction in terms. All the more, is it so with those who lead God's people without prayer. It has been well-said that what a minister is in his prayer closet before God alone is what he is—nothing more, nothing less. This is why the enemy would have pastors do a hundred different wonderful things, if he can stop them from praying. Spiritual leaders can only minister effectively when we pray consistently.

Likewise, spiritual leaders must be devoted to public prayer. It is the job of pastors-teachers to lead the people of God in prayer. The proclamation of the word is the most public thing pastors do. And we are most often judged by our preaching and teaching. But this text places prayer right alongside of the ministry of the word. It indicates that spiritual leaders are to be just as committed to leading the church to pray as we are in leading the church in the ministry of the word. All that we do in the name of Christ is to be fueled by believing prayer. Much prayer; much power. Little prayer; little power. No prayer; no power! The apostles understood that spiritual leaders must lead in and through prayer.

Likewise, spiritual leaders must be devoted to the ministry of the word. Acts 6:1-7 is often considered to be the formal institution of the ministry of deacons in the church. But the text itself never indicates that this is what was going on. The word "deacon" is not used in this text. Its related term "ministry" is used in the text. But it does not apply the office of deacons. And it is not used to describe the seven men selected to wait tables. It is used in verse 4 to describe the work of the apostles. They were devoted to "prayer and the ministry of the word." This is the role of the spiritual leaders of the church. Every Christian is a minister of Christ. Spiritual leaders serve Christ as ministers of the word.

This was not just the calling of the apostles. It is the calling of all who would exercise spiritual oversight over God's people. In 2 Timothy 4:1-2, Paul writes, "I charge in the presence of God and of Christ Jesus, who is to judge the living and the dead, and by his appearing and his kingdom: preach the word, be ready in season and out of season, reprove, rebuke, and exhort with complete patience and teaching."

Many people think pastors-teachers do very little work. They think we just play golf all week and get up when it's time to preach and let it rip. Those who do that are not true men of God. Indeed, some men make their pulpit work look so easy that you would think that it did not cost them any effort. But they have to work hard to make it look easy. The faithful ministry of the word requires preparation as well as proclamation. Bible exposition does not grow on trees. God does not speak to preachers and supernaturally give them the exegesis of the text. 2 Timothy 2:15 says, "Do your best to present yourself to God as one approved, a worker who has no need to be ashamed, rightly handling the word of truth."

One more thing: Let me spotlight an obvious but overlooked standard of spiritual leadership in this text. This passage makes it clear that Christ exercises pastoral oversight of his church through a plurality of godly men. This point can be made from virtually any passage in the New Testament that discusses spiritual leadership. But notice that this point is made in the text before us. Acts 6 records the selection of the first leaders outside of the apostles. And the church was to select seven men. While these seven men made sure the needs of the widows were met at the daily distribution of food, the twelve would devote themselves to prayer and the ministry of the word. This is a reminder that the church is not to be a one-man show.

Christ alone is to be preeminent in the church. And we must not allow any cult of personality to develop around any particular leader. There ought to be a plurality of godly men in the church who are qualified, able, and ready to lead the church in prayer and the ministry of word.

The Strategy and *Power* of Racial Unity

Verses 5 reports, "And what they said pleased the whole gathering, and they chose Stephen, a man full of faith and of the Holy Spirit, and Philip, and Prochorus, and Nicanor, and Timon, and Parmenas, and Nicolaus, a proselyte of Antioch." The seven names listed in verse 5 are all Greek names. These were Hellenistic men. It was the neglected Hellenists who began to complain. And in the providence of God, seven Hellenists were chosen to make sure the resources were allocated to meet the needs of the widows. This problem was being resolved in a way that would dramatically signify that protecting turf was not to get in the way of meeting needs.

Verse 6 says, "These they set before the apostles, and they prayed and laid their hands on them." In so doing, the twelve affirmed these chosen men before the entire church. The reference to the laying on of hands does not suggest the impartation of a special gift, unction, or ability. The fact that they went through the screening process of the saints was proof that they had what they needed for the task. They had a good reputation, were filled with the Holy Spirit, and conducted themselves with spiritual wisdom.

Verse 7 is one of the periodic progress reports of the gospel Luke gives in Acts: "And the word of God continued to increase, and the number of the disciples multiplied greatly in Jerusalem, and a great many of the priests became obedient to the faith." This summary statement reports the results of the apostolic strategy, congregational cooperation, and ministry appointments described in the previous verses. It also gives us the proof of a growing church: "And the word of God continued to increase."

This expression of church growth is quite different from how we often think of church growth today. In far too many instances, we measure churches in terms of how many people attend, how many programs they offer, or how much money they raise. We celebrate size, money, facilities, influence, and prominence, even when these celebrated churches do not demonstrate submission to the authority of God's word or confidence in the sufficiency of God's word. But this verse reminds us of the true evidence of a growing church—the word of God increases!

My father's friend, a fellow pastor in Los Angeles, Dr. E. V. Hill, led my father's funeral. And he led my installation service at the church. Mind you, I was seventeen years old—a senior in high school—when I was called to pastor the church. Dr. Hill gave a classic E. V. Hill sermon.

First of all, he gave opening remarks for twenty-five minutes. (I do not advise, young preacher, that you do that.) And then he said, "Well, I guess I'll get on to the message now." Dr. Hill just wanted to address that elephant in the room—my age. He said, "I want to talk tonight from the subject: *What can that boy tell me?* That's the question we need to ask tonight. He's only seventeen years old. What can that boy tell me when my marriage is in trouble? What can that boy tell me when my child has gone astray?"

He took passage after passage out of the Old Testament and the New Testament to affirm the sufficiency of God's Word. He ended by declaring, "He could tell you whatever the Word of God tells him to tell you."

This is the critical matter of our day, friends: *Does the church truly have confidence in God's Word?* God's Word has the power to save the lost, to nurture the church, to counsel the troubled, to change lives, to reach the culture. Do you believe that? Prayer really is a God-given means by which he accomplishes his sovereign purposes. Do you believe that?

May we devote ourselves to prayer and the ministry of the Word. May we lift this scandalous gospel of a blue-collar worker from an ancient ghetto called Nazareth who was actually God in the flesh and came to earth to die at the cross to pay for our sins, and who rose from the dead with all power in his hands. And if you run to the cross and repent of your sins and trust the blood and righteousness of Jesus Christ, you can have free forgiveness, new life, and eternal hope. To the glory of God.

Therein lies the answer for racial reconciliation—trust in and the genuine pursuit of obedience to the Word of God and prayer. The gospel is sufficient, but it must be our all-consuming priority.

Verse 7 reports that as the word of God increased, the number of disciples multiplied! And the last line of verse 7 specifies a particular group of people who were becoming obedient to the faith: the priests. In Acts 4, the priests and the other religious authorities showed up at the temple as Peter and John were teaching the people and proclaiming in Jesus the resurrection from the dead. They arrested, threatened, and beat Peter and John for the bold witness of Christ. The priests were vehemently opposed to the message of Christ. If Christ was the true Lamb of God that takes away the sins of the world, the priests were out of business. So they worked hard to undermine the gospel in Jerusalem. But when the church made sure that the main thing remained the main thing, the word of God increased and even caused many of the priests to put their faith in Jesus as Savior and Lord. Let the church be the church, and the Lord will send revival and restoration that will change lives in our cities and throughout the nations.

THREE

THE PEACEFUL SOLUTION TO RACIAL UNITY

H. B. Charles Jr.

Therefore remember that at one time you Gentiles in the flesh, called "the uncircumcision" by what is called the circumcision, which is made in the flesh by hands—remember that you were at that time separated from Christ, alienated from the commonwealth of Israel and strangers to the covenants of promise, having no hope and without God in the world. But now in Christ Jesus you who once were far off have been brought near by the blood of Christ. For he himself is our peace, who has made us both one and has broken down in his flesh the dividing wall of hostility by abolishing the law of commandments expressed in ordinances, that he might create in himself one new man in place of the two, so making peace, and might reconcile us both to God in one body through the cross, thereby killing the hostility. And he came and preached peace to you who were far off and peace to those who were near. For through him we both have access in one Spirit to the Father. So then you are no longer strangers and aliens, but you are fellow citizens with the saints and members of the household of God, built on the foundation of the apostles and prophets, Christ Jesus himself being the cornerstone, in whom the whole structure, being joined together, grows into a holy temple in the Lord. In him you also are being built together into a dwelling place for God by the Spirit. (Ephesians 2:11–22)

I began my first pastorate at the age of seventeen, a senior in high school. I did not, however, learn to drive until I was 19 years old. For several years, family, friends, and church leaders drove me everywhere.

At some point, one of the church leaders could not take it anymore. Brother Tibbs called and asked if I would go somewhere with him the next morning. He did not tell me where. The next morning, Tibbs arrived at my apartment. I followed him out to the driveway to find a driving instructor waiting for me. When I completed the driving course, Tibbs took me to a local DMV to get my driver's license.

The day I got my driver's license, I also bought my first car—a Volkswagen Passat. The date was April 29, 1992. But I don't remember the date merely because it was the day I got my driver's license and first car. The events that unfolded that day in my city mark it as an unforgettable day for the entire nation.

That Wednesday evening, I led prayer meeting and Bible study at my church, which was located in Midtown area of the city. Afterwards, I was scheduled to preach a revival in Compton, which was on the other side of town.

As I sat in my church study preparing for the evening assignments, I took a break and turned on the news to catch up on current events. I was saddened but not surprised to see that a jury in Simi Valley acquitted four Caucasian police officers for the videotaped beating of African-American motorist Rodney King.

Transfixed with the news, I could not get back to work. Then there was more breaking news. As I watched a live feed of impromptu protests on the corner of Normandy and Florence, four black youth yanked truck-driver Reginald Denny from his cab and viciously beat him in the street. I had to turn the TV off. It was all too much to take in.

I finally pulled myself together to teach my congregation. But I advised members not to join me for the later service, as planned. I thought it was best that they go straight home. I was right.

I drove to Compton to preach, with a few friends in tow. It was an adventure, as the day I got my driver's license and first car was also the first time I drove the freeways of Los Angeles. After the service, one of my passengers joked that the ride home would not be as adventurous as the drive to church. But none of us were prepared for what happened next. When I entered the freeway onramp, the night sky was filled with flames of fire everywhere we looked. The Los Angeles riots had begun.

By the time this terrible riot was finally over, 53 people were dead, 2,383 persons were injured, more than 7,000 fires were started, and some 3,100 businesses were looted, including virtually all the businesses in the community near where our church met on Gramercy Place. The city suffered more than $1 billion worth of destruction.

Rioting stopped when the government sent military into the city to regain order. But in the minds of many, the real turning point was when Rodney King—the man at the center of the controversy—addressed the public in a press conference. He was obviously nervous, overwhelmed, and at a loss for words. In the midst of his stammering remarks, King made the quote for which he is remembered. It was a question. "Can we all get along?"

Rodney King is now dead. But his question lives on. *Can we all get along?* Personal problems, family issues, racial divisions, urban challenges, political infighting, international conflict, terrorist threats all around us beg that question—Can we all get along? Is true peace possible? What does it take for love to conquer hate? For unity to replace division? For kindness to bring an end to hostility?

The apostle Paul answers that all-important question for us in Ephesians 2:14-18. Here, the word of God makes it clear that only Jesus Christ can bring peace with God and with one another.

There are three fundamental reasons why we should look to the Lord Jesus Christ for peace. (1) Jesus Christ *is* our peace; (2) Jesus Christ has made peace for us; and (3) Jesus Christ preaches peace to all.

Jesus Christ *Is* Our Peace

Ephesians 2 is about the saving gospel of Jesus Christ. In verses 1–10, the apostle describes salvation in personal terms. In verses 11–22, Paul describes salvation in cultural terms. In verses 1–10, he shows us how the Lord makes Christians. In verses 11–22, he shows us how the Lord made the church.

Verses 11-13 directly address Gentile readers in the church of Ephesus. In verses 11-12, Paul exhorts his readers to remember what they were before salvation:

> Therefore remember that at one time you Gentiles in the flesh, called "the uncircumcision" by what is called the circumcision, which is made in the flesh by hands—remember that you were at that time separated from Christ, alienated from the commonwealth of Israel and strangers to the covenants of promise, having no hope and without God in the world.

Then verse 13 shifts the readers' focus from the past to the present. "But now in Christ Jesus you who once were far off have been brought near by the blood of Christ." Paul tells the church to remember what you were before Christ (verses 11-12). Then he tells the church to recognize what you are in Christ (verse 13).

Then, in verses 14–18, Paul explains the process that transformed the readers from what they were to what they are. A radical transformation has taken place through Christ, who is our peace.

Peace in the Person of Christ

First of all, there is peace in the *person* of Christ. Micah 5:5 records a prophecy about the coming Messiah-King. "And he shall stand and shepherd his flock in the strength of the Lord, in the majesty of the name of the Lord his God. And they shall dwell secure, for now he shall be great to the ends of the earth. And he shall be their peace." In Ephesians, Paul declares this messianic promise is fulfilled in the Lord Jesus Christ. *He himself* is our peace. Jesus is the source of spiritual peace. Jesus is the embodiment of divine peace. Jesus is the personification of true peace. The prophet Isaiah rightly calls this one who will be born King, the "Prince of Peace" (Isaiah 9:6).

How can we find peace for the racial divisions that separate us? For that matter, how can we find peace in any sphere of life? Answer: Jesus Christ. He himself is our peace. There is no peace to be found anywhere else or in anyone else. It is Jesus only and only Jesus. He, and he alone, is our peace.

In the Upper Room, Jesus said to his grief-stricken disciples, "I have said these things to you, that in me you may have peace. In the world you will have tribulation. But take heart; I have overcome the world" (John 16:33). Jesus Christ is our peace. He is the only one who can bring peace, reconciling man to God and man to man.

In Psalm 34:11–14, David sings:

Come, O children, listen to me;
    I will teach you the fear of the LORD.
What man is there who desires life
    and loves many days, that he may see good?
Keep your tongue from evil
    and your lips from speaking deceit.
Turn away from evil and do good;
    seek peace and pursue it.

Notice what the psalmist says. "Do you want to live a good life? Then seek peace and pursue it." But where should you seek peace? Where can peace be found? In Ephesians 2:14, Paul states that life's elusive peace is found in the Lord Jesus Christ.

As a black man in America, I am the beneficiary of those who have marched, protested, and even rioted for the sake of civil rights. My father was among those who stood up and sat in to be treated fairly. I am grateful. Yet human activism will never change sinful hearts, as the aftermath of the Civil Rights movement has demonstrated. The only way there will be peace among the races is through Jesus Christ. He himself is our peace. Different races, local churches, and family members cannot truly be at peace with one another through self-effort. We must believe the word of God that declares there is peace in the person of Christ.

Peace in the Work of Christ

Second, we see there is peace in the work of Christ. Again, verse 14 asserts: "For he himself is our peace, who has made us both one and has broken down in his flesh the dividing wall of hostility."

There are two aspects of the work of Christ that produced peace. First of all, Christ is our peace, *because he is the one who has made us both one.* Jews and Gentiles were separated from one another, alienated from one another, hostile toward one another. But in Christ these polarized groups have become one. How did this happen? It did not happen by merely making the Gentiles a part of Israel. And it did not happen through some separate-but-equal coexistence. *He has made the two one new man.* R. Kent Hughes writes: "Jesus didn't Christianize the Jews or Judaize the Gentiles. He didn't create a half-breed. He made an entirely new man."[3] The two have become one.

Paul wrote to the churches of Galatia, "For as many of you as were baptized into Christ have put on Christ. There is neither Jew nor Greek, there is neither slave nor free, there is no male and female, for you are all one in Christ" (Galatians 3:27-28). Racial dynamics, gender differences, or cultural issues do not define us as Christians. In Christ, we have become a whole new race. He has made the two one.

It is often said that blood is thicker than water. That's generally true. But it is not true if that water is Christian baptism. Think about it. In Christ, we are closer to one another than to an identical twin, if that person does not trust Jesus Christ as Savior and Lord. Christ has made us one. He has created a new man, a new community, new race of people, called the church.

Not only has Christ made us one, he has also broken down the dividing wall of hostility (Ephesians 2:14). The temple complex had various courts. One court, the Court of the Gentiles, was the only place in the temple complex where Gentiles were allowed. A dividing wall, as it were, separated Jews and Gentiles. But Christ has broken down, in his flesh, the dividing wall of hostility that separated us.

---

3   R. Kent Hughes, *Ephesians: The Mystery of the Body of Christ*, Preaching the Word (Wheaton, IL: Crossway, 1990), 91.

After the resurrection of Jesus Christ, when he was raised from the dead after paying for our sins at the cross, the temple complex with its courts and walls were still standing. When Paul penned these words to the Ephesians, they yet remained. So this statement cannot ultimately be about a physical structure. It is about a spiritual attitude. Hostility in a person's heart against another can build high walls without brick and mortar. But the redemptive work of Christ at the cross tore down this wall of hostility. Jews and Gentiles were hostile toward one another. It was a high wall of division. But Jesus Christ broke it down.

How did Christ tear down the wall? Paul says he did it "in his flesh" (Ephesians 2:14). This is a reference to both the incarnation and cruci-fixion of our Lord. By his blood-soaked cross and his empty tomb, Christ has broken down the dividing wall of hostility. Shame on us for building up what Christ by his death at the cross has broken down!

In 2015, our predominantly black Baptist congregation merged with a predominantly white Baptist congregation. It was a big step of faith that garnered a lot of press. Several years into this gospel journey, I am often asked, "What have you learned?"

Good question.

The first thing I would say I have learned is that people are people. Plain and simple. People are people. We are all sinners. All of us are in des-perately need of the grace of God. Everyone meets Christ from a place of weakness, not a place of strength.

I have learned something else during this process. Our recently-merged congregations are able to practice unity to the degree we focus on Christ, keep the gospel first, and let the Word of God have the last say. Without a doubt, the proclamation of the Word of God and the testimony of Jesus Christ has joined our hearts and minds together as one.

However, to the degree we have allowed secondary things—like min-istry programs, music styles, church structures, even sanctuary seats—to become primary, we inevitably see corresponding degrees of division.

The truth is that it is impossible for us to be one if we are focusing on anything but the Lord Jesus Christ. As we lift up Christ, proclaim his sav-ing work, and fellowship around the word, we are privileged to see how the gospel of Jesus Christ does exactly what Paul is saying here—tears down walls of hostility. Jesus Christ is our peace.

Jesus Christ Made Peace for Us

But also consider with me the fact that Jesus Christ made peace for us. In verse 14, Paul declares that Christ is our peace. At the end of verse 15, he shifts to say the one who is peace has also made peace. In verses 15 and 16, we see three ways Christ has made peace for us.

Through the Law

How did Christ make peace for us? Verse 15 says, "by abolishing the law of commandments expressed in ordinances." This is the only place the terms "law," "commandments," and "ordinances" are used in the same verse. It is an emphatic reminder that God has a righteous standard no one can reach. Romans 3:23 says, "for all have sinned and fall short of the glory of God."

We have broken God's law. We have disobeyed God's commands. We have violated God's ordinances. But Jesus abolished the law of commandments expressed in ordinances. In Matthew 5:17, Jesus said, "Do not think that I have come to abolish the Law or the Prophets; I have not come to abolish them but to fulfill them." Jesus did not abolish the law in the sense of rendering it meaningless. He moved it out of the way by fulfilling the righteous standards of the law. Christ lived the righteous life we should have lived. And he died the death we should have died, making atonement for our sins. In Romans 10:4, Paul writes, "For Christ is the end of the law for righteousness to everyone who believes."

By the Blood of the Cross

Why did Christ make peace for us? Verses 15-16 state, "that he might create in himself one new man in place of the two, so making peace, and might reconcile us both to God in one body through the cross, thereby killing the hostility." Christ has made peace for us by reconciling us both to God. 1 Timothy 2:5 says, "For there is one God, and there is one mediator between God and men, the man Christ Jesus."

Christ reconciled us both to God in one body. Verse 16 tells us the means by which Christ did it—"through the cross." Colossians 2:13-14 says, "And you, who were dead in your trespasses and the uncircumcision of your flesh, God made alive together with him, having forgiven us all our trespasses, by canceling the record of debt that stood against us with its legal demands. This he set aside, nailing it to the cross." We broke God's law. And God had our rap sheet. But he nailed it to the cross. And the blood of Jesus covers our sins to reconcile us to God in one body. William MacDonald rightly commented, "The cross is God's answer to racial discrimination, segregation, anti-Semitism, bigotry, and every form of strife between men."

In the Church, as One Body

What is the proof that Christ has made peace for us? Verses 15-16 say, "that he might create in himself one new man in place of the two, so making peace, and might reconcile us both to God in one body through the cross, thereby killing the hostility." The proof that Christ has made peace for us is that he has made us "one body." In Ephesians 4:4–6, Paul declares, "There is one body and one Spirit—just as you were called to the one hope that belongs to your call—one Lord, one faith, one baptism, one God and Father of all, who is over all and through all and in all."

We are one in Christ. Verse 16 says he killed the hostility. This tells us what the barrier to peace among people is: sin. Adam and Eve were naked and unashamed. But when they sinned, they started hiding from God and one another. Sin separates us from God and from one another. But Christ has killed the hostility. This is why the church ought to be characterized by peace. The cross binds us together. So we must not build any dividing walls of hostility in the church or allow any to stand. Marriages end over so-called "irreconcilable differences." But is there any such thing as an irreconcilable difference if Jesus has killed the hostility between us? So it is with the church!

How can the church let things like personal tastes, music styles, program preferences, non-essential traditions, selfish ambition, or interpersonal conflict divide us if Christ has killed the hostility between us? For Christ's sake, we must tear down any dividing walls of hostility among us.

A minister cared for young boys in his orphanage, and during their bus rides racial tensions would arise. All of the black kids would sit on one side, and the white kids would sit on the other side. The tension broke out one day, and he in frustration pulled the bus to the side of the road, marched them all off, and gave them a stern lecture. When he finished, his concluding thought was that there is no more black and white in this orphanage. "Everyone," he said out of frustration, "from now on is green." Then he put them back on the bus. When he started driving again, he heard somebody murmur in the back, "Dark green on the left and light green on the right."

This is just how we are as sinners. We find a way to divide. This is why we desperately need the gospel. Not just the gospel for the world around us, but *we* need the gospel. We need to be reminded of what we were without Christ and what we are in Christ.

Jesus Christ Proclaims Peace to All

There is peace in the *person* and *work* of Christ. But verses 17-18 tell us there is also peace in the message of Christ.

We receive the message of peace through Christ. Verse 17 reads, "And he came and preached peace to you who were far off and peace to those who were near."

When did Christ preach peace? The obvious answer is during his earthly ministry. But that does not seem to be what Paul is saying here. Christ occasionally ministered to Gentiles. But his earthly ministry primarily focused on the lost house of Israel. Furthermore, if it was during his earthly ministry, on what basis did Christ preach peace? Verses 14-16 are clear Christ made peace by the death he died after the life he lived.

Verse 17 most likely points beyond the crucifixion and resurrection of Jesus to the ministry of the early church. In a real sense, this is an affirmation of the Great Commission. "All authority in heaven and on earth has been given to me. Go therefore and make disciples of all nations, baptizing hem in the name of the Father and of the Son and of the Holy Spirit, teaching them to observe all that I have commanded you. And behold, I am with you always, to the end of the age" (Matthew 28:18-20).

The main question of verse 17 is, to whom did Christ preach peace? Verse 17 answers, "And he came and preached peace to you who were far off and peace to those who were near." The Gentiles were far off. In verse 13, Paul writes: "But now in Christ Jesus you who once were far off have been brought near by the blood of Christ." The Gentiles were far off. The Jews were near. But Christ came and preached peace to both. This is a subtle but powerful affirmation of sovereign grace. In Romans 1:16 Paul writes, "For I am not ashamed of the gospel, for it is the power of God for salvation to everyone who believers, to the Jew first and also to the Greek." But here Paul reverses the order and says Christ preached peace to those who were far off and to those who were near.

This verse reminds us that sin places us all on an equal level. It is like the days of Noah. Some people lived on high mountains, others in low valleys. But when the rains fell and the floods rose, everyone died in the floodwaters that did not have a ticket to ride with Noah on the good ship grace. So it is in Christ. It does not matter if you are near or far. If you are in Christ, you are saved, safe, and secure.

Remember the parable of the Prodigal Son in Luke 15:11-32. The overtly rebellious son was lost in the far country. And the self-righteous son was lost in the back yard. One was far, and one was near. Yet both sons needed to be reconciled to their loving father. So it is in Christ. Some have wasted their lives in nightclubs. Others have wasted their lives on church pews. But far is not too far. And near is not close enough. The ground is level at the foot of the cross.

We enjoy the privilege of peace through Christ. The Bible teaches that God is one in essence, three in person—God the Father, God the Son, and God the Holy Spirit. It is not easy to understand how three equals one. Try to explain it and you'll lose your mind. Try to explain it away and you'll lose your soul.

The word "Trinity" is not in the Bible. But the truth absolutely is. Verse 18 is clear evidence of the triunity of God. "For through him we both have access in one Spirit to the Father." Through God the Son both Jews and Gentiles have access in God the Holy Spirit to God the Father. All three members of the Godhead were at work to make Jews and

Gentiles a new race of people called the church. God the Father planned it. God the Son accomplished it. God the Holy Spirit sustains it.

The key word of verse 18 is "access." It means "to bring near." It was used of the privilege of having an audience before a superior. The Greek term was the title for the person who would introduce visitors to a ruler in the ancient world. But here the focus is on the result, not the process. Christ's work is the believer's privilege.

The sinner's dilemma is that he or she has no access to God. Ephesians 2:12 says, "remember that you were at that time separated from Christ, alienated from the commonwealth of Israel and strangers to the covenants of promise, having no hope and without God in the world." But Ephesians 3:12 says in Christ "we have boldness and access with confidence through our faith in him." Let us work, worship, and witness to spread the good news of reconciliation to this divided world.

The last battle of the American Revolution was the Battle of Blue Licks. But it was a battle that should have never been fought, for it was fought after the war was over! News traveled slowly. There was no means of quick communication over the Appalachian Mountains to Blue Licks, Kentucky. The two sides went on fighting because no one knew the war was over. Lost people are at war against God and against one another, because they do not know that the battle is over because of the finished work of Christ. May the Lord use us to get the good news out that the Lord Jesus Christ is our peace!

Under the Blood—We Are All Rednecks

When we were in discussions at Shiloh Church with the Ridgewood Church about the possibility of us merging our works together, I went to the Ridgewood Church and met with the membership for a question-and-answer period.

One of the last questions I got was from an old brother who stood up in the back and said, "Well, Brother Pastor, I don't have a question about what's about to happen. But I do have one concern, and I know you're going to be the new man in charge and you can do whatever you want to—but I was just curious that once you're in charge, will you still let us have the Beast Feast?"

I said, "Excuse me?" Pastor leaned over and explained to me the Beast Feast, that every summer the brothers killed wild game, cooked it up, and had a fellowship where they just ate beast. And someone would give a gospel testimony. As a father of three children, I knew just how to answer this: "We'll see."

But afterward, he came up to me and said, "Pastor, I wasn't trying to put any pressure on you, it's just I've led that Beast Feast for these eleven years, and every year we've seen somebody come to Christ. That's why I hope you'll consider doing it. Because I'm sure," he said, "Pastor, you would agree with me that if one redneck comes to Jesus, it's worth it all."

I agreed. I went out to my car and the elders were there, and I told them the story. They didn't believe me. I said, "There is the brother right there." And I said, "Come here, brother. Tell them what you just told me." And he confidently, joyfully repeated everything he had said to me.

We all had a good laugh, but when we finished he said as he walked away, "But remember pastor, covered by the blood of Jesus we are all rednecks." I got what he was trying to say. In his own colloquial way, he was saying what Paul is saying to us. *Christ is our peace. Christ has made peace for us. Christ preached peace to those who are near and to those who are far.* To the glory of God.

FOUR

THE COSMIC PURPOSE FOR RACIAL UNITY

Juan Sanchez

Not long ago I sat on a panel with a very well-known author who has a multiethnic congregation. He's doing a lot of great work, planting different churches. At some point, the question of racial reconciliation came up, and he said, "I hear people saying, 'All you need is the gospel!'" He seemed frustrated that we have an issue of this magnitude, and that somehow people would think the gospel simply is going to take care of it.

Now in part, I understand what he's saying. Formulaic or simplistic answers will never penetrate the depths of what is wrong in our world. But the gospel in action is neither formulaic nor simplistic. The gospel is the only means of genuine reconciliation. Apart from the gospel, we can't be reconciled to God, and we can't be reconciled to one another. Perhaps there is some relative good that can be done in our culture and in society, but I'm afraid that apart from the gospel, the best we can do is approach a measure of civility.

Paul's letter to Ephesians reveals the roadmap to the unity the church needs. In Ephesians 1, Paul explains this wonderful salvation we have, and he discloses God's eternal plan. In Ephesians 1:7–9 he says: "In him [Christ] we have redemption through his blood, the forgiveness of our trespasses, according to the riches of his grace, which he lavished upon us, in all wisdom and insight making known to us the mystery of his will."

When Paul uses the word "mystery," he means something that was formerly hidden but is now revealed. In other words, it's not something that just showed up. It's been there all along. So, Paul says in 1:9–10, "making known to us the mystery of his will, according to his purpose, which he set forth in Christ as a plan for the fullness of time." That means this is God's eternal plan that was to be revealed at the precise moment of God's intention. And here is God's intention—"to unite all things in him, things in heaven and things on earth."

God's Eternal Plan

So, what is God's eternal plan? In a nutshell, God's eternal plan is to exalt his Son Jesus Christ as King and Lord over all, and to unite all that has been fractured by sin in Christ and to place everything under Christ.

We see this plan as we come to 1:16–18. Paul says, "I do not cease to give thanks for you, remembering you in my prayers, that the God of our Lord Jesus Christ, the Father of glory, may give you the Spirit of wisdom and of revelation in the knowledge of him, having the eyes of your hearts enlightened." Paul wants them to know and understand this mystery:

> That you may know what is the hope to which he has called you, what are the riches of his glorious inheritance in the saints, and what is the immeasurable greatness of his power toward us who believe, according to the working of his great might that he worked in Christ when he raised him from the dead and seated him at his right hand in the heavenly places, far above all rule and authority and power and dominion. (Ephesians 1:18–21)

When Paul uses that language of "rule and authority and power and dominion," he's talking about the angelic, and even demonic realm. God the Father has placed Jesus far above "all rule and authority and power and dominion, and above every name that is named, not only in this age but also in the one to come. And he put all things under his feet and gave him as head over all things to the church, which is his body, the fullness of him who fills all in all."

When you study the image of God in Genesis 1, you begin to see that God's plan was to have a human king rule over his creation, a king who would represent his rule on the earth and display the glory of God. Adam failed. Israel as a nation was to display the glory of God by representing his rule on the earth, showing all the nations what God was like, what his kingdom was like, what it was like to live under him. Israel failed.

Jesus is the true image of God. He is the one who reveals what God is like, and he is the one who inaugurates the kingdom of God so that now, through Christ, we are incorporated into this body. Ephesians 2:1–10 explains how we come into this body through salvation by God's grace alone, through faith alone, in Christ alone. And then, picking up in verse 11 we see the reality of what God is doing. He is creating this one new man, Jew and Gentile. In chapter 3, God displays his manifold wisdom through this church.

In his letter to the Ephesians, and in chapter 3, in particular, Paul argues that the gospel gives us our hope. The gospel gives both the racist and the victim hope. Apart from the gospel, there is no hope. And the reality of this hope displays the cosmic purpose of God's redemptive plan. In Ephesians 3:1–6, Paul says he has received a revelation from God by God's grace.

The Gospel Revealed

Being entrusted with the gospel implies stewardship. Paul was a prisoner: physically, literally. But in Ephesians 3:1 he says that in a metaphorical sense, he is a prisoner for Christ on behalf of the Gentiles. Then in verse 2, interrupting his thought, he writes, "assuming that you have heard of the stewardship"—he's a manager—"of God's grace that was given to me for you, how the mystery was made known to me by revelation, as I have written briefly."

Paul was not sitting in Starbucks creatively doodling on a napkin, trying to figure out what message would revolutionize the world. This gospel was *given* to Paul. It was revealed to him—a "mystery" that was always there, formerly hidden but now revealed. He explains the content of this mystery in Ephesians 3:6: "This mystery is that the Gentiles are fellow heirs, members of the same body, and partakers of the promise in Christ Jesus through the gospel."

Now this is revolutionary. Israel was supposed to relate to the nations in two ways. They were to display to the surrounding nations who their God was, what he was like, what it is to live in his kingdom under his rule, and what it was to be citizens of his rule. Anyone who wanted to come under God's rule and be incorporated into his people could be. So, we know of Ruth. We know of Rahab. It didn't seem to happen often in Scripture, but if you were willing to become a Yahweh worshiper, be circumcised (males), and enter into the covenant, you could be part of the people of God.

But Israel failed in its representation of God. Eventually the prophets began proclaiming a message that God is going to do something new. There's going to be a new exodus so magnificent that it will cause people to forget the first one. And Jesus Christ is the one the prophets spoke of, the answer to the exile. Thus, Matthew's Gospel begins with Jesus as the answer. Jesus retraces Israel's steps. And Jesus is the one who leads God's people out of exile once and for all.

Israel was to function as a light to the nations, but now a mystery has been revealed: Gentiles are included in the redeemed people of God. But that's not a completely new revelation, because the second way that Israel is to relate to the nations is through an end-time ingathering. The prophets speak about a time when Israel will bring in the nations to God.

This mystery that's been developing in the Old Testament has now finally come to full fruition. Now we see that through Christ, through the Jewish Messiah, all who have faith in him are included in the people of God. The Gentiles are fellow heirs. Believing Gentiles receive the same inheritance as believing Jews. Both are members of the same body. Both are partakers of the same promise in Christ Jesus through the gospel.

This is good news. This is good news for all. We are united to one another, Jew and Gentile as one people, one body, one church. It is in Christ, through the gospel, that Jews and Gentiles share in the Abrahamic promises of worldwide blessing. This is the same gospel that saved us, and this is the same gospel we're called to preach.

But apart from Christ there is no hope. The gospel has been revealed. The church is built on the foundation of the apostolic witness to Jesus Christ, that in Christ the promises of the new covenant of forgiveness of sin, the promise that people would have a personal knowledge of God, the promise that God's Spirit would dwell in us—that promise is available to all who believe in Jesus Christ. And that's why it's called good news.

The Gospel Proclaimed

But notice, it's not enough just to know the gospel. We must proclaim the gospel. And so, in Ephesians 3:7–9, we see this gospel proclaimed. Paul says he was made a minister of this gospel by the grace of God in verse 7. "Of this gospel I was made a minister according to the gift of God's grace, which was given me by the working of his power." Paul doesn't claim any credit for the gospel or the knowledge of this gospel. He doesn't claim any credit for the ministry that he has. It is all from God, and it is all for God.

In verses 8–9, Paul explains his ministry in two parts. First, he says: "To me, though I am the very least of all the saints, this grace was given, to preach to the Gentiles the unsearchable riches of Christ." Paul makes this mystery known to Gentiles by preaching the gospel to them *and inviting them into the people of God through Jesus Christ.* In verse 9 Paul reveals the second aspect of his ministry: "and to bring to light for everyone what is the plan of the mystery hidden for ages in God, who created all things."

If I were to ask you the question, What is the eternal plan of God? what would you say? Ephesians 1:7–10 reads: "In him we have redemption through his blood, the forgiveness of our trespasses, according to the riches of his grace, which he lavished upon us, in all wisdom and insight making known to us the mystery of his will, according to his purpose, which he set forth in Christ as a plan for the fullness of time, to unite all things in him, things in heaven and things on earth."

Ephesians 1:22 says, "And he [God] put all things under his [Christ's] feet and gave him as head over all things to the church, which is his body, the fullness of him who fills all in all." Thus Paul's ministry is to tell Gentile believers that (1) they are participants in the vast wealth of the Jewish Messiah and (2) he is bringing to light the eternal plan of God to unite all things in Christ and to place all things under Christ.

The privilege of evangelism is that you are actually participating in God's eternal plan to show everyone Jesus Christ is King and Lord. The gospel has been revealed so that it might be proclaimed. But it doesn't stop at proclamation.

The Gospel Displayed

In Ephesians 3:10, Paul gives the purpose of his ministry. He says, "so that through the church the manifold wisdom of God might now be made known to the rulers and authorities in the heavenly places." I take this to be not just the angelic host, but I think also this includes the demonic realm as well.

In other words, when Jew and Gentile, black and white, male and female, Asian and Hispanic, are brought together under Christ through the gospel together, we are displaying God's glory to the heavenly realm and saying, "Our God is unimaginably wise, and powerful, and gracious. Our God is holy—there is no one like him."

The world celebrates diversity. But the Bible does not celebrate diversity per se. The Bible celebrates *unified diversity*. In other words, the miracle of the gospel is not simply a diverse crowd. You can go to a football game and see black, white, Asian, Hispanic all wearing the same color. You can gather a diverse crowd around classical music or jazz. You can gather a diverse crowd around food or wine. But the gospel doesn't merely gather a diverse crowd. It gathers a diversity *and makes us one*.

This unity from diversity is what displays the wisdom of God. In fact, Revelation 7:9–10 reads: "After this I looked, and behold, a great multitude that no one could number, from every nation, from all tribes and peoples and languages, standing before the throne and before the Lamb, clothed in white robes, with palm branches in their hands, and crying out with a loud voice, 'Salvation belongs to our God who sits on the throne, and to the Lamb!'" These are the saints in heaven before God praising God for the salvation that he has granted them. But notice what happens next. It says, "And all the angels were standing around the throne and around the elders and the four living creatures, and they fell on their faces before the throne and worshiped God, saying, 'Amen! Blessing and glory and wisdom and thanksgiving and honor and power and might be to our God forever and ever! Amen.'"

It is an amazing truth that God displays his manifold wisdom through the church when we come together as this multiethnic, multicultural community—and we function as one. This unity glorifies God because it shows to the heavens the wisdom of our God in salvation, that he alone is powerful. He alone is wise in bringing people from formerly hostile parties and causing them to be together as one. This unity doesn't merely apply to some universal or even theoretical concept of the church. It is displayed in local churches. It happens as we seek to display the manifold wisdom of God together, and as we evangelize.

We should be careful not make a multiethnic church our idol. But here's what I believe: if you and I in our churches are practicing Ephesians 3:8–9, we ought to pray that Ephesians 3:10 would result. If we are being faithful to proclaim the gospel in our neighborhoods, in our community where our church is, in our workplace, where we recreate, where we shop, when we get together as family—we ought to pray that our church would eventually come to reflect the diversity of the community that we're in. So, if your community is not very diverse, you won't display much diversity. But there's more than just ethnic diversity. There's socioeconomic diversity. There's educational diversity. There's generational diversity. There's all kinds of diversity.

For too long the church has adapted the homogenous unit principle, where like attracts like, and we've thought, "Well, if we want to attract young people then we have to be young." And pastors older than I am are wearing ripped jeans and ripped T-shirts, and I'm thinking, "What are you doing?"

This is not particularly complicated. It is extremely difficult, but the principles are not overly complicated. Let me ask it this way: Do you know people who are different from you? Do you know unbelieving people who are different from you? Are you praying that God would give you opportunities to have gospel conversations with those people who are different from you?

When the Lord chooses to save through our multicultural evangelism, there will be much that we have to work through in light of these varied cultures. We need to keep asking the question, How can we as a church display the manifold wisdom of God? This passage has caused me to rethink ethnic-language church planting. It's caused me to rethink how we do things as a church. You see, it's not mere diversity that glorifies God. It's a unified diversity, which is why Paul in Ephesians 4 begins to talk about unity:

> I therefore, a prisoner for the Lord, urge you to walk in a manner worthy of the calling to which you have been called, with all humility and gentleness, with patience, bearing with one another in love, eager to maintain the unity of the Spirit in the bond of peace. There is one body and one Spirit—just as you were called to the one hope that belongs to your call—one Lord, one faith, one baptism, one God and Father of all, who is over all and through all and in all. (Ephesians 4:1–6)

We are to display that people from hostile parties can come together and function in love. The gospel brings together fractured marriages. The gospel brings together fractured families. The gospel brings together a fractured humanity, because it is the eternal plan of God to exalt his Son Jesus Christ as Lord and King and to unite all things in him. The gospel that has been revealed and proclaimed will only be displayed if God's people choose to live in light of the unifying power of the gospel.

The Gospel Practiced

Here's the bottom line: when we come together as a church, we need to understand that it's not about what we do in the realm of social reform. It's not about all the external issues that arise from different cultures and backgrounds. It's about preaching the gospel of Jesus Christ, which unites us and leads us to love one another in self-sacrificial love, so that we don't demand our personal preferences. That's how we must live together as a church and fight together as a church.

We have to get to know one another. We have to take time to know the people around us, the people in our neighborhoods, the people we don't know. We need to work at it. And we need to do it with gentleness and humility. We need to be willing to ask questions. We need to be willing to think the best of others. We need to be willing to give the benefit of the doubt. But beloved, the gospel unites us. That is the reality.

As Paul says in the rest of chapter 4, through the ministry of the gospel we go from being children to being adults. That's what the ministry of the Word does. It continues to work in us, and it continues to mature us as we hear the Word, and as we speak the Word to one another. So, the gospel that has been revealed is the gospel that we must proclaim. And this gospel that is proclaimed, when it does its work, is displayed in the local church. And it shows that our God is wise in placing his Son as King and Lord over all things. We are participants in a cosmic display of God's glory in heaven and on earth.

May our Lord grant us the grace to embrace our role in this drama, so as not to be ashamed at the finale.

FIVE

THE PRACTICAL PLAN FOR RACIAL UNITY

Juan Sanchez

The church I pastor is very multiethnic and multicultural. We have African Americans, Africans, Asians, Hispanics, Anglos, and so it's a very diverse congregation. Politically, there's a lot of diversity as well. The tension created by this multiculturalism became real for us in the 2016 presidential election. My main concern as a pastor was to maintain the unity of the Spirit and the bond of peace for our congregation. To me, that was of utter importance. It didn't matter who got elected. Our main focus was to make sure we were speaking to each other in a way that honors everyone and helps us understand that no matter what is going on outside, the world can't tear us apart. It can't divide us. We sought to follow God's plan for unity.

As we saw in the previous chapter, Paul's letter to the Ephesians reveals the roadmap to the unity the church needs. It reveals that the miracle of the gospel is not diversity. *The miracle of the gospel is a unified diversity*. The world craves diversity. The world celebrates diversity. You can go on any university campus and they're celebrating diversity. But what is spectacular, what is unbelievable about the gospel, is not that you have people from every tribe and nation and language and people *together in salvation*. What is miraculous about the gospel is that all these people are *actually brothers and sisters in Christ and are to function as a family.* That's the miracle of the gospel.

Based upon the foundation he has laid in Ephesians 1–3, Paul deals in chapters 4–6 with *how* people from different languages, different tribes, different nations, and different cultures begin to walk as a family that glorifies God. Ephesians 4:1 serves as the theme sentence for the rest of the letter: "I therefore, a prisoner for the Lord, urge you to walk in a manner worthy of the calling to which you have been called." Paul is talking about our manner of life. The "calling to which you have been called" summarizes chapters 1–3. Considering God's glorious redemption, and cosmic purpose for that redemption, we are to glorify him by our walk, by our life together as a church.

Walk in Unity

First, we need to walk in the unity of the Spirit, with all humility and gentleness (4:1–2). How many problems could be solved if we dealt with people in humility and gentleness, and didn't immediately assume the worst of people? We need to look for evidences of grace in other people's lives. We need to humble ourselves. We have to practice self-control, not just in our speech, but also in our Facebook posts, in our tweets, and on Instagram. Unfortunately, on social media we don't have the immediate discomfort that we normally would in person. As a Latino, that's hard for me to do. I speak first and then I think. We live in a dangerous place, in a dangerous time, where we don't walk in much humility. We're not very gentle people.

But because we have been saved by God's grace through faith in Christ, we're to walk in a manner worthy of that calling, with humility and gentleness. This can be difficult. Driving, waiting in line—anything involving other people—exposes our lack of humility, lack of gentleness, and lack of patience. We have a sinful proclivity for self-preference—to make everything about us. You know, my drive to the office is about me and you're in my way. When we're impatient with our children, what we're saying is, "Look, my time is more important than your time, so come on. Let's get with it." You know, when we give an instruction to our child and they don't do it right the first time, our impatience shows something about us.

The gospel changes our self-ward trajectory. We have a new heart. We have God's Spirit. This is what Paul is saying. In fact, notice what he goes on to say in verses 2–3: "bearing with one another in love, eager to maintain the unity of the Spirit in the bond of peace."

Paul is saying: "Look, this is not your unity. You didn't make this unity up. This unity is a gift. This is the unity of the Holy Spirit, and you're to maintain it." Instead of fighting for our preferences, we're to fight for the unity of the Spirit in the bond of peace.

How often do we actually fight for unity—which means a denial of self? Sometimes we seek compromise. "Okay, I'll meet you halfway." But self-denial is not something we often fight for. We need to consider how the gospel has changed us, and we need to renew our minds. We need to stop thinking like the person we were in Adam, and we need to start thinking as the person we are in Christ.

And this is the ground of our unity in Christ: "There is one body and one Spirit—just as you were called to the one hope that belongs to your call—one Lord, one faith, one baptism, one God and Father of all, who is over all and through all and in all" (Ephesians 4:4–6). We're to fight for that unity. We're to be eager to maintain that unity. We're to deny self. We're to be patient with people. Yet we all know that these are hard things to do in our own strength.

Thankfully, Jesus doesn't just make demands and say, "Okay, you're on your own. Pull yourself up by your own bootstraps." But the ascended Christ has structured his church in such a way that we would grow in this unity and mature in this unity. When we bicker and fight, when we argue, and when we're impatient, it reveals our childishness. But Jesus Christ has structured his church so that all of us would be able to mature into this very image of Jesus Christ.

In verse 7 Paul confirms that this unity does not mean uniformity. He says, "But grace was given to each one of us according to the measure of Christ's gift." So we're to be eager to maintain the unity of the Spirit in the bond of peace, but the reality is that we all have different gifts. Even though we're to be united, there is diversity within the body.

Again, diversity is a beautiful thing, but our diversity is not like the world's. The world can have a diversity by gathering people around a sport, gathering people around food. We are united because we have been gathered around Christ and his gospel. And the ascended Christ didn't leave us to our own devices. Paul says in verse 8 that Jesus Christ is victorious. He has ascended. He has gained captives. "And he gave gifts to men." In verse 9 Paul adds, "In saying, 'He ascended,' what does it mean but that he had also descended into the lower regions, the earth?" I think here Paul is simply talking about Christ's incarnation. Then he continues, "He who descended is the one who also ascended far above all the heavens, that he might fill all things."

In other words, the eternal plan of God was to exalt his Son Jesus Christ as King and Lord over all. He descended from heaven. He fulfilled his ministry. Now he's ascended to the right hand of the Father, where he is ruling on high as King of kings and Lord of lords. And God is placing every enemy under his feet. But notice that the point here is that he gave gifts to men:

> And he gave the apostles, the prophets, the evangelists, the shepherds and teachers, to equip the saints for the work of ministry, for building up the body of Christ, until we all attain to the unity of the faith and of the knowledge of the Son of God, to mature manhood, to the measure of the stature of the fullness of Christ, so that we may no longer be children, tossed to and fro by the waves and carried about by every wind of doctrine, by human cunning, by craftiness in deceitful schemes. Rather, speaking the truth in love, we are to grow up in every way into him who is the head, into Christ. (vv. 11–15)

Jesus has structured his church for this very life together. He has given the church ministers of the Word. In the context of Ephesians, I take "apostles and prophets" to be the New Testament apostles and the New Testament prophets—those to whom this gospel has been revealed and now serve as the foundation of the church. We see in chapters 2–3 that the foundation upon which the church is being built is the apostles and the prophets, Jesus Christ being the chief cornerstone. Then you seem to have these evangelists who propagate this gospel, and shepherds and teachers who build up these churches in a local setting.

Notice verse 12: "to equip the saints for the work of ministry, for building up the body of Christ." So the purpose of the ministers of the gospel, the ministers of this Word, is to equip the church "for the work of ministry, for building up the body of Christ, until we all attain to the unity of the faith and of the knowledge of the Son of God, to mature manhood, to the measure of the stature of the fullness of Christ" (vv. 12–13).

So, how does this growth happen? This is really important—it happens through the sufficiency of God's Word. Here's what we see in verses 14–15: Rather than listening to every wind of doctrine, human cunning, craftiness, and deceitful schemes, "speaking the truth in love, we are to grow up in every way into him who is the head, into Christ."

As we're growing up into Christ, growing in oneness with Christ, we are to be growing in oneness with one another. We are growing up from childhood to adulthood in Christ. We're not tossed about by every latest doctrine that comes down the pike. But how this happens is that in God's grace, the ascended Christ has gifted the church with ministers of the Word who preach the Word, who teach the Word, who share the Word. And then this Word reverberates through the congregation so that the church speaks this very Word to one another in love, with the result that we're all building up one another in love. Jonathan Leeman has a book called *Reverberation* where he explains this process.

Think of the beauty of the ministry of the Word of God in the local church. The pastor is a gift of the ascended Christ to the local church. He prepares and he preaches the Word. As he preaches the Word, that Word is received. And then believers begin to speak that truth in love with their children, around the lunch table, at home, or at a restaurant. They begin to share that Word with other church members, maybe in a Sunday school class or in a Bible study. And notice what happens: "speaking the truth in love, we are to grow up in every way into him who is the head, into Christ, from whom the whole body, joined and held together by every joint with which it is equipped, when each part is working properly, makes the body grow so that it builds itself up in love" (vv. 15–16). The maturing process is at work.

This is what we're called to do. We're called to speak the truth of God's Word to one another in love. We're called to apply this gospel to one another's lives. We want to develop a culture in our congregations where people are reading the Word together, where we're speaking the Word to one another, where we're praying together, where we have the kind of community and the kind of unity and the kind of relationships where people can say important things, even hard things, to one another.

Do you have anyone in your church whom you allow to say hard things to you? Do you have anyone in your life that you allow to say, "Hey, how are you doing? Are you okay? I've noticed some things that I'd like to talk to you about." Do you have someone in your life that can speak to you in those ways? This is what we call the culture of discipleship. A culture in which the Word is preached, or the Word is taught in a Sunday school class, and then it reverberates throughout the congregation, and we're speaking that Word with one another.

This is the wisdom of the plan of the ascended Christ. He is still shepherding his church through his Word, and through his human shepherds. These human shepherds too are sheep. And together, the sheep speak this Word to one another, so that we're growing up and we're encouraging one another to be gentle and humble. We're encouraging one another to be patient.

That's how we're to function as the church—we are a family. I don't know about your family, but in my family things are sometimes a little messy. If church is family, church sometimes is a little messy as well. But we must understand that we're all growing. We haven't grown up. We've not come to mature adulthood. We're all growing, and we need each other to grow. That's why the local church is so important. The church is not some man-made concoction. This is Jesus's plan to shepherd his sheep and display the glory of God. He has structured his church for this kind of ministry: to walk in the unity of the Spirit in the bond of peace. But as I've stated previously, this is a unique unity.

Walk in Holiness

In verses 17–24 Paul tells us we are to walk not only in unity but also in holiness. I'm stating that positively, but Paul actually states it negatively. He says, "Don't walk like the pagans walk."

> Now this I say and testify in the Lord, that you must no longer walk as the Gentiles do, in the futility of their minds. They are darkened in their understanding, alienated from the life of God because of the ignorance that is in them, due to their hardness of heart. They have become callous and have given themselves up to sensuality, greedy to practice every kind of impurity. But that is not the way you learned Christ!—assuming that you have heard about him and were taught in him, as the truth is in Jesus, to put off your old self, which belongs to your former manner of life and is corrupt through deceitful desires, and to be renewed in the spirit of your minds, and to put on the new self, created after the likeness of God in true righteousness and holiness.

The apostle is essentially saying: "You're a Christian, so act like a Christian. You're no longer a pagan; you're no longer an unbeliever, so stop acting like an unbeliever and start acting like who you already are in Christ." He picks up in verses 25–29:

> Therefore, having put away falsehood, let each one of you speak the truth with his neighbor, for we are members one of another. Be angry and do not sin; do not let the sun go down on your anger, and give no opportunity to the devil. Let the thief no longer steal, but rather let him labor, doing honest work with his own hands, so that he may have something to share with anyone in need. Let no corrupting talk come out of your mouths, but only such as is good for building up, as fits the occasion, that it may give grace to those who hear.

How powerful would it be if in our conversations we spoke words that built up instead of words that tore down? With our children. Children with parents. And the church with one another.

Notice what Paul is saying. We're to walk in a manner worthy of this calling, in unity, in holiness, distinct from the world. Our temptation is to be accepted by the world. That's why young people have such a hard time, because they want to be accepted by the world. But the way to overcome that struggle is to understand you have been accepted by God through Christ. No greater value has been attached to you. There's no greater dignity. There's no greater name than to be a child of God. You don't have to seek acceptance from the world, because God in Christ has accepted you.

We're to live together as a church, reminding one another of this holiness. We're to encourage one another toward this holiness. We're to have these kinds of conversations. Our congregations need to be the kinds of cultures where things like this can take place. But Paul reminds us that holiness is also kind and tender, and forgiving. "And do not grieve the Holy Spirit of God, by whom you were sealed for the day of redemption. Let all bitterness and wrath and anger and clamor and slander be put away from you, along with all malice. Be kind to one another, tenderhearted, forgiving one another, as God in Christ forgave you" (vv. 30–32). These verses serve as a transition of sorts. We're to walk in unity. We're to walk in holiness. And, we're to walk in love.

Walk in Love

Ephesians 5:1–2 reads: "Therefore be imitators of God, as beloved children. And walk in love, as Christ loved us and gave himself up for us, a fragrant offering and sacrifice to God." If our attitude was to walk in the self-sacrificial love of Christ, how would our homes change? How would our workplaces change? How would our churches change? What would happen when we dealt with other people we love in a self-sacrificial way, not looking out for our best interests, but looking out for the interests of others? Now, these are not all strictly sequential. We don't have to walk first in unity, then holiness, then love. They are all inextricably bound together, as the phrase "walk as children of light" in verse 8 and the following exhortation, from verses 3–6, demonstrate.

But sexual immorality and all impurity or covetousness must not even be named among you, as is proper among saints. Let there be no filthiness nor foolish talk nor crude joking, which are out of place, but instead let there be thanksgiving. For you may be sure of this, that everyone who is sexually immoral or impure, or who is covetous (that is, an idolater), has no inheritance in the kingdom of Christ and God. Let no one deceive you with empty words, for because of these things the wrath of God comes upon the sons of disobedience.

Notice his distinction between the children of disobedience and the children of light.

Therefore do not become partners with them; for at one time you were darkness, but now you are light in the Lord. Walk as children of light (for the fruit of light is found in all that is good and right and true), and try to discern what is pleasing to the Lord. Take no part in the unfruitful works of darkness, but instead expose them. For it is shameful even to speak of the things that they do in secret. But when anything is exposed by the light, it becomes visible, for anything that becomes visible is light. Therefore it says,

> "Awake, O sleeper,
>   and arise from the dead,
> and Christ will shine on you."

I think that's pretty self-explanatory, isn't it? We're not to walk like the world. We're to walk as the children of light because we have been brought out of darkness into the light in the Lord Jesus Christ. We are to walk in holy love, which is informed by God's wisdom.

Walk in Wisdom

Again, unity, holiness, and love are facets of the same spiritual diamond:

Look carefully then how you walk, not as unwise but as wise, making the best use of the time, because the days are evil. Therefore do not be foolish, but understand what the will of the

Lord is. And do not get drunk with wine, for that is debauchery, but be filled with the Spirit, addressing one another in psalms and hymns and spiritual songs, singing and making melody to the Lord with your heart, giving thanks always and for everything to God the Father in the name of our Lord Jesus Christ, submitting to one another out of reverence for Christ. (Ephesians 5:15–21)

And then Paul unpacks what that submission looks like—wives to husbands, slaves to masters, children to parents. In other words, we as the church are an embassy of the kingdom here on this earth. Jesus Christ is our King. We are his ambassadors. And as we live life together as church, the world is watching us. When they look at us, they should see a beautiful and glorious Christ, and they should see the joy of the kingdom. When they look at us and see this unified diversity, they should want to know how is it that these people who used to hate each other can now come together. How is it that this husband and wife who were on the verge of divorce, their life has been transformed? How is it that this family that was falling apart has been put together? How is it that former cultural enemies have become partners in faith in service to Christ?

It is not easy, and it's not over till we die or till Jesus returns, but that's what the church ought to look like. It is what the church needs to pursue. This is what it means to live together as a church. It's a glorious vision, isn't it? And in light of our focus in this book, it is God's practical plan for racial unity.

SIX

THE MINDSET FOR RACIAL UNITY

Danny Akin

Let me describe a bit of my history. My grandfather was a member of the Ku Klux Klan. I experienced integration in the fifth grade, the same year Martin Luther King Jr. was assassinated. I grew up in a wonderful church. I was called into the ministry from that church. A few years after my call to ministry, I learned that the pastor had wanted to invite E. V. Hill to come and preach in our church, but tragically, the deacons voted it down. He was not extended an invitation.

That was the world in which I grew up. And yet, at the same time, I was blessed to have grandparents and then parents, in particular my mother, who taught me that's not the way you think. It's not the way that you act or treat other people.

Today, I'm blessed to be part of a seminary that has as one of its core values "kingdom diversity." One of the things I've learned over the last several years is those of us who are white, who have not grown up in a minority context, we just need to be quiet, listen, and learn. We tend to talk too much. And because we often talk so much we don't get to hear other people's stories. We don't get to appreciate their perspective.

Another thing I've learned is you won't be kingdom diverse by accident. You must be intentional.

The message of Philippians 2 is crucial to achieving racial reconciliation and a unified diversity. Paul says, "So if there is any encouragement in Christ, any comfort from love, any participation in the Spirit, any affection and sympathy, complete my joy by being" (1) "of the same mind," (2) "having the same love," (3) "being in full accord"—literally of one soul—and (4) "of one mind" (Philippians 2:1–2). He goes on in verses 3–11:

> Do nothing from selfish ambition or conceit, but in humility count others more significant than yourselves. Let each of you look not only to his own interests, but also to the interests of others. Have this mind among yourselves, which is yours in Christ Jesus, who, though he was in the form of God, did not count equality with God a thing to be grasped, but emptied himself, by taking the form of a servant, being born in the likeness of men. And being found in human form, he humbled himself by becoming obedient to the point of death, even death on a cross. Therefore God has highly exalted him and bestowed on him the name that is above every name, so that at the name of Jesus every knee should bow, in heaven and on earth and under the earth, and every tongue confess that Jesus Christ is Lord, to the glory of God the Father.

There are three movements to our text. In verses 1–5, we're going to examine the character of Christ. In verses 6–8, we're going to examine the cross of Christ. And then finally, in verses 9–11, we're going to examine the crowning of Christ.

The Character of Christ

Paul begins by challenging us in verses 1–4 to cultivate the character of Christ. And being a good teacher, Paul begins by noting in verse 1 a number of divine blessings that are true for every child of God: "So if there is any encouragement in Christ," if there is "any comfort from love," if there is "any participation"—that is, if there is any fellowship—"in the Spirit," and if there is "any affection and sympathy"—or mercy.

The word "if" does not connote doubt. Paul uses it as a literary device to emphasize his point that these blessings are ours. If you belong to Jesus, if you have been united with Christ, then there are four realities that are true for you and for me.

Paul was in prison when he wrote the letter to the Philippians, not knowing exactly what the future held for him. He was hopeful that he would be released, and we know from other records that he was. But he at this time he didn't know for sure what the future held.

Though Paul did not know what was going to happen to him—and he knew he might actually face execution—he still had comfort. He says in essence, "I am comforted because I know that Jesus loves me."

But then he says, "If there is any . . . participation [or fellowship] in the Spirit." I think Paul may have in mind the fact that the Philippians had ministered to him time and time again, which resulted in this participation in the Spirit within the body of Christ. Then he says that for everyone who belongs to Jesus, there is "affection and sympathy," or affection and mercy. He begins in verse 1 by laying a foundation of blessings, then in verses 2- 4 he begins to admonish them and challenges them based upon these 4 blessings in verse 1.

In verse 2, the divine behavior—Christlikeness, having the mind of Christ—is characterized by unity. In verse 3, it is characterized by humility. And then in verse 4, it is characterized by sensitivity.

A Life Characterized by Unity

Paul begins by saying that our lives are to be characterized by unity. In verse 2 he says, "Complete my joy." Make me a happy apostle. How? By doing four things: (1) "being of the same mind," (2) "having the same love," (3) "being in full accord," and (4) being "of one mind."

It would seem likely that if everybody had been getting along, if everybody had been unified, if there were no issues in the church, Paul would have had no reason to write verse 2. But he did write it, and he reinforces it four times: be of the same mind, have the same love, being in full accord, be of one mind.

Now, why does he need to do that? In this wonderful, mission-minded church of Philippi, there were two ladies that were now engaged in a catfight. On one side, you had this lady named Euodia, and very clearly she had her followers and defenders. On the other side of the church, there was a lady named Syntyche, and she also had her followers and supporters.

These two women at one time had been active in the gospel and in ministering alongside Paul. But something had happened, and now they were at odds with one another. People were beginning to follow one or the other, and the church was on the verge of being divided.

So Paul writes in 4:2: "I entreat Euodia and I entreat"—I *plead* with—"Syntyche to agree in the Lord." Indeed, he then in verse 3 asks the church to get involved. "Yes, I ask you also, true companion, help these women, who have labored side by side with me in the gospel together with Clement and the rest of my fellow workers, whose names are in the book of life."

We need to be reminded that we are different, we are going to see things differently, and, if we're not careful, we can allow healthy differences to become carnal differences. We can begin to allow our differences to influence us more than our unity in Christ.

Furthermore, there's a very interesting phrase in 2:2 that I always draw attention to at least for my own well-being and edification: "having the same love." One of the miracles of the gospel is that God can enable us to love people we don't like—to love people we don't get along with.

Now, maybe you're reading this and you say, "Oh, but Brother Danny, I like everybody." And I would say to you, in my most gentle, gracious, southern Georgia voice, "You are a liar." Because nobody likes everybody. Nobody.

In fact, God has given me the joy over the last twenty-five years to be an administrator in a Southern Baptist seminary. And I can say with an absolutely honest heart that I have loved every single student God has sent to either one of those schools I served. But I must also confess to you that there are some of them that when graduation day came, I was more than thrilled to give them back to you all because you sent them to me, and now I got to give them back. They rubbed me the wrong way. They were high maintenance. They caused difficulties. They whined. They complained. And when graduation day came, I was so glad that they would be leaving.

But I can say this to you: I've never had a student that I could not say before the Lord, "Lord, I love that student, and Lord, in spite of the fact that I may not like the way they act all the time, I want you to bless them. I want you to use them. I want them to soar for your glory."

God enables us supernaturally to love people that in our flesh we would not want to be around.

A Life Characterized by Humility

In Philippians 2:3, the apostle calls for humility: "Do nothing"—not a single thing—"from selfish ambition or conceit," (or perhaps better, "vain conceit").

Selfish ambition is an attitude that says, "I must have what I want. It doesn't matter who gets run over. It doesn't matter who gets knocked down or hurt. I must have what I want." Vain conceit adds to that, "I deserve what I want. I'm the smartest. I'm the best. I work the hardest. I see things from the best perspective."

Now, before I move on, let's be very spiritual for just a moment. How many of us really want what we deserve? "God, I want what I deserve. Give it to me." I'll be honest: I don't want what I deserve because I know that I deserve to die and go to a place called hell—and to spend all of eternity there separated from God.

No, I don't want what I deserve. I want what God's amazing grace through Jesus has provided. So when I relate to God based on grace, why would I not also turn and relate to others in that kind of way?

A Life Characterized by Sensitivity

In Philippians 2:4 the idea comes full circle: "Let each of you look not only to his own interests, but also to the interests of others." From the Greek term for "look" here, we get the words "telescope" and "microscope." The idea is scope out the interest of others.

In other words, Paul would say when you begin each day, you don't begin with you. You begin with God. "Lord, how might I this day honor you and please you and serve you?" And then others: "Lord, how might I this day serve others—my wife, my children, my church, my neighbors, the lost?"

When you see the mind of Christ in action, you see people being treated like Jesus would treat people, you see a church thinking about people like Jesus thought about people, and you see people serving people like Jesus served people. Which leads us to the heart of this beautiful hymn found in verses 6–11.

The Cross of Christ

Verse 6: "who, though he was in the form of God." That phrase "form of God" means nature or essence of God. Paul is simply saying this: whatever it is that makes God God—Jesus is all of that. If God is all-powerful, all-knowing, everywhere present; if God is holy, just, righteous, immutable, and eternal—God the Son, the Lord Jesus, the incarnate God is all of that. He existed and has always existed in the form of God. But he "did not count equality with God a thing to be grasped." In other words, he did not consider his equality with God something he had to reach for as if it wasn't his, because it was his. Nor did he hang onto it as if it was something that could be taken from him. After all, you can't steal deity from deity.

So he did not count his equality with God as something that he would use for his own advantage or his own privilege. No, he did exactly the opposite of that. He emptied himself.

This does not mean that somehow he laid aside his divinity. The incarnation was not a subtraction of deity. It was an addition of humanity (not sinful humanity like you and I have, but like that of Adam and Eve before the fall). A sinless humanity. Notice the words of Jesus's high priestly prayer in John 17:5, "Father, glorify me in your own presence with the glory that I had with you before the world existed."

In the incarnation, he did not set aside his deity, but for a brief period of time he did lay aside his glory. In the incarnation, the Son of God, the Lord Jesus became God incognito. When you just looked at him, at first glance you thought you were simply looking at a man. But if you listened more carefully and looked more intently, you would recognize deity in the flesh.

Philippians 2:7 tells us that Jesus emptied himself "by taking the form of a servant." He did so by "being born in the likeness of men. And being found in human form." He did so by humbling himself. He did so "by becoming obedient to the point of death." He did so by submitting even to "death on a cross."

Theologians have often referred to this as the Great Condescension. Think about it. God the Son is in heaven and he comes to earth, but he doesn't stop there. He comes to earth and he becomes a man, but he doesn't stop there. He becomes a man who becomes a servant. But he doesn't stop there. He becomes a servant who dies, but he doesn't even stop there. He becomes a servant who dies the most shameful, the most humiliating death known in the first century. He dies the death of a cross.

The great Roman orator Cicero said that death by crucifixion was indeed so shameful and so humiliating that a Roman citizen should never speak of it. He went on to say a Roman citizen should not even think of it.

The Crowning of Christ

In the very best sense of the phrase, the Lord Jesus Christ "went all the way" for you and for me. And because he chose to come down, God then in response raised him up. Note the movement from humiliation in verses 6–8 to exaltation in verses 9–11: "Therefore God has highly exalted him." This could be translated "super-exalt," "exalt to the highest possible place," or "exalt in the highest possible way." And God "bestowed on him the name that is above every name."

Now, contextually you would draw the conclusion that the name God bestows is Jesus. Theologically, you might be more prone to say that the name he is given is the name Lord. Personally, I don't think you have to make a distinction between the two.

In verse 10, Paul says that "at the name of Jesus that every knee should bow." This is Paul's shorthand for every tribe, every tongue, every people, and every nation. Every knee should bow "in heaven and on earth and under the earth." Believers and angels in heaven, believers and unbelievers on earth, and every demon including Satan himself is going to bow the knee to Jesus.

Mark it down, your knee is going to bow and you are going to confess that Jesus Christ is Lord to the glory of God the Father. It is going to happen either in this life or at the judgment, but every knee is going to bow.

I have a dear friend who is an atheist. I've known him now since about 1990. I still pray for him. We still correspond. He hasn't come to faith in Christ. But he spent six months in our college going to systematic theology classes, going to New Testament survey classes, as well as a class in philosophy and ethics.

At the end of six months of classes, he was going back to Manhattan, New York, where he lived. He would write a book called *Chapter and Verse: A Skeptic Revisits Christianity*. It's a really good book. It's very fair, very honest. I mean, he basically said: I spent six months with evangelicals. You know what? They're not a bunch of whack jobs. I mean they're actually pretty smart. And he said they can give good answers for why they believe what they believe.

And he said in that book: they have something I don't have. In fact, he said in essence at the end of one chapter: Let's just be honest. From my worldview perspective, life's a dog (he used a different word there); life's a dog and then you die.

You know what? If there's no God, he's probably right. He came to visit our house right before he left. At the end of our conversation, I said, "Well, Mike, I just have one question: what's the bottom line in all of this?" He said, "That's easy, Danny. It's the resurrection."

I said, "I would agree with you." I said, "Why do you say that?" He said, "Well, it's easy. If Jesus of Nazareth rose from the dead, there are a number of things that are clearly self-evident and true." He said, "(1) There's a God. (2) Jesus is that God. (3) The Bible is true because Jesus believed the Bible was true. And that means (4) heaven and hell are real. And (5) your relationship with him makes all the difference."

And I said to him, "That's pretty good theology." He said, "Well, I had some good teachers." I said, "Well, fine. So tell me, what happened on the first Easter morning? I mean, after all, you don't believe it." He said, "Well, I'm an atheist. I don't even believe there's a God. How can I believe in a resurrection?"

I said, "Well, fine. I think you care about me." He said, "Oh, I love you. I love you and your family." I said, "Well, I believe that. I really do.

But you also think I'm some crazy, wild-eyed fundamentalist who doesn't really have a clue about what the real world is like." And he said, "Oh, I don't believe that." I said, "Oh, yes you do. Be honest. You think that I've bought the farm in terms of my intellectual credibility." He said, "You're right. I do."

I said, "Fine. I'm glad we can be honest. So I need you to help me out. What do you think happened on the first Easter morning?" And I'll never forget what he said as long as I live. He said, "I don't know." He said, "I don't know."

I said, "What do you mean you don't know?" He said, "Well, I've studied this quite a bit. I admit, there's a lot of evidence for an empty tomb." He said, "Danny, I'm an atheist. I don't even believe there's a God. And so I guess I'll just have to suspend my judgment for now."

Especially at that time in my life—I was in my thirties—I wasn't highly emotional. But tears began to run down my face. I looked at my friend and I said, "You know, I would hate to think that you're going to die and go to hell over suspended judgment."

And then I said, "You know, Mike, I don't think the problem is in your head. Intellectually, you know the evidence is there. The problem is in your heart. You don't want to bow the knee and submit to Jesus as your Lord."

He said, "Danny, you may be right. Don't stop praying for me." Now I find that fascinating that an atheist would say to me, "Don't stop praying for me." I haven't stopped praying, and I'm still asking God to open his heart, breathe in new life, so that he will bow the knee and not at the judgment, but with great joy and delight of his soul in worship to Jesus as Lord.

When you really, truly understand the implications of what it means to bow before Jesus as Lord, you cannot help but see people like Jesus sees people. You cannot help but think about people in the way Jesus thinks about people. And you cannot help but treat people like Jesus treats people.

The character of Christ is manifest in people who embrace the cross of Christ and exult in the crowning of Christ.

My mother was probably the godliest person I've ever known. She was so much like Jesus in so many ways. I can remember when I was in high school, a friend of mine named Danny Pounds was walking to a football game.

Danny Pounds was a young black man about sixteen years old, big guy, about six foot four, 225 pounds. But he had torn up his knee, and so he had a walking leg cast on. He was about three-quarters of a mile from the high school. My mother, by herself, was driving to come watch me play. She saw Danny walking along the sidewalk. She stopped and pulled over and said, "Danny, get in the car. Let me drive you on to the ballgame. You don't need to walk that far."

And so my little five-foot-four white mother has a six-foot-four, 225-pound black man in the front seat with her and she drives on up to the game. When they got there, Danny very politely said, "Thank you, Mrs. Akin. Very kind of you to do that." And he began to walk in one direction. Somebody that saw what had happened, a friend of my mother's, came over and said, "Emma Lou, have you lost your mind? Why in the world would you pick up that boy and give him a ride?" My mother, with the most simple, honest, pristine answer, simply said, "Because he needed one."

You see, because she saw Danny like Jesus sees Danny, she treated Danny like Jesus would treat Danny.

We see from Philippians 2:1–11 that the character of Christ is manifest in people who embrace the cross of Christ and exult in the crowning of Christ. This is the path to racial unity and reconciliation. Jesus' people are called to have the mindset of Christ—which is the mindset for racial unity.

SEVEN

THE RADICAL ELEMENT IN RACIAL UNITY

Carl A. Hargrove

How do we define racial unity? What is racial reconciliation? Racial reconciliation and racial unity must be defined under the integrity of the gospel. We can have genuine racial unity only insofar as we submit to the principles taught in God's Word. First, we must submit to the reality that God is the Creator of all men. Second, we must submit to the reality that no man is better than the other because we are all image bearers. Third, we must recognize that, as the church, we are joined in a dynamic relationship with the living God, because God has reconciled us to Christ and brought us into one family, one faith. Only when these three truths are embraced can we begin to think about genuine racial unity and reconciliation.

Now the ground that we, in fact, have in common is that we are all dead in our sins from birth, and separated from God. There must be a reconciliation that takes place with the divine Creator and his creatures. That can only take place through the person of the Lord Jesus Christ. When we think about reconciliation, it must be under the integrity of the gospel. And at the heart of the gospel is forgiveness.

A Complex Problem? Yes and No

Though many would desire to make racial disunity too complex for such a "simplistic" solution, believers understand that God's Word is sufficient— the gospel of Jesus Christ is truly enough to overcome the intricate maze of sin that makes up race relations in a fallen world.

That's the beauty of God's Word, isn't it? Either directly or by way of principle, God's Word will guide us through the treacherous waters of life's decisions. We, as the church, must speak to racial disunity and disharmony. We must speak to bigotry and mistrust. Simply put, we must address the issue of sin that is behind these problems. We cannot be silent on racism while speaking against other manifestations of sin in society. This is not a simply a social issue, but a concern of the heart that requires the input of the those with lasting solutions to have their voice heard in the conversation.

But I also think that it's important to see how this sin manifests itself. The big picture *is* sin. Because all men and women are sinners, there will be prejudice and bigotry. We understand that, but that's the shotgun approach. How can we take a bit more of a sniper's approach at addressing the problem? Shouldn't can we deal with the nuanced roots involved in the sins of bigotry, racism, and disunity? When we speak against adultery, we are obligated to address greed, pornography, selfishness, bitterness, pride, among other vices which contribute this sin. So we should do the same with the sin of racism and disunity.

When it comes to sins of racial disunity, there are issues of bitterness that people have in their heart because of some genuine hurt—or, at times, simply a perceived hurt. But they've allowed either real or perceived offenses to sink into their hearts and grow into bitterness. That bitterness doesn't know how to discern between those people who are genuinely at fault and those who are not, so they just put everyone together. They become bitter toward an entire people group.

My father honorably served in WWII and Korea, yet he returned to a country that denied him privileges and rights that should have been afforded any citizen, and all the more, someone who was willing to pay the ultimate price for his country. However, in my conversations with him concerning racism, I never received from him a message of bitterness. He would speak frankly about injustices which were evident to all, while balancing those conversations with stories of men he served under during this time in the Army and the kind acts of civilians in the States. He was free from the crippling effects of a bigoted society.

Experiences expressed by my father or other instances come by way of cultural insensitivity, institutional racism, and personal grievances. And then there is that overarching sin, which is the sin of pride. We all struggle with it. At times, our pride says to one person, "I am better than you are. We are better than you are." That's because we have not submitted to God's revelation that says God is the Creator of all, and we are all image bearers. And so, in sin, we create this false narrative that the unbelieving world reinforces and inflames. The white supremacists and neo-Nazis naively but dangerously believe in their supremacy over non-Aryan people. This incessant pride in its many forms, even outside the camp of racist organizations, is the heart of racial disunity.

What we face today isn't new. Jesus told the parable of the good Samaritan because of a hardness of heart that manifested itself in cultural superiority. In John 4, Jesus had to go through Samaria because he had an appointment with a Samaritan woman at a well. Since the sin of man's pride at Babel, man has been divided. Although one may biblically say that there is only one race, there are still divisions based on our present definition of race, and there are undoubtedly divisions based on class and culture.

We must recognize that race is not always the cause of disunity between classes and cultures. These distinctions are much deeper than the color of one's skin. Some of the most significant atrocities in history have been perpetrated by man against his fellow man—among people who looked the same, except they had distinct cultural/tribal differences. Mankind has demonstrated this in Africa, Europe, and Asia. Actually, no continent has escaped making distinctions, although some have the escaped the more regrettable horrors of attempted genocide, prejudice, injustice, and systemic oppression.

My wife, who is Korean, has said there are cultural differences among Korean peoples that have at times culminated in one group viewing itself as superior to another. No matter the ethnicity, there are divisions—within the so-called races, and between the so-called races.

In some cases, people hold things against other people they don't even know. How can I have anything against you without knowing you? How can you have something against me without knowing me? We don't know what others have faced in life. How can we say, for example, that some have privilege because they're of a particular race? Anybody from any race might have been an orphan, an abused child, come from a broken home, or consistently told they would never amount to anything. Sometimes we assume these things as we live our lives in these relationships that are flawed even at best.

This is not to say that class systems have not created more opportunities for others, but we must be careful before we judge an entire people group. We must seek to know each person as an individual first if we are to strive for reconciliation. The problem is at the same time complex and simple. The problem is sin—but that sin has a web as diverse as the number of sinners manifesting their prejudices in varying contexts.

A Radical Solution

So, what is the solution? It's as radical as basic Christianity. Live the Christian faith before a broken and dying world. Live in view of the radical reconciliation that has occurred between you and God because of the gospel. If we can live out basic Christianity, which really is terribly profound, then that will affect our relationship with each other, with our neighbors, and then it cannot help but have a lasting effect on society as well.

I believe that it's important to understand that unbelievers can achieve some measure of unity based on our common humanity. Unbelievers can achieve a better marriage, unify behind a common cause (sports, humanitarian causes, political ideologies), and demonstrate genuine acts of valor. History has shown that people will at times unify for a common cause, one that might even cost one's life.

The unity of genuine believers goes beyond what the unbelieving world can imitate. It is based on a common redemption, and a common Redeemer—a common faith in the one who justifies though we were previously united only in our ungodliness and spiritual death. Only born-again believers—the true church—understand radical, underserved forgiveness and reconciliation. The unity of believers is grounded in grace and forgiveness. It is a forgiveness that seeks the best for others. Though we can't fully grasp how offensive our sins were or are to a holy God, grace is our motivation. We too, therefore, are called and compelled by grace to learn to forgive others, though they do not really understand the depth of their offenses. Grasping this reality will help the church live in racial unity, and strive to exemplify it for those outside the church.

Without forgiveness, there can be no reconciliation with God, and unless there is forgiveness among men there can be no reconciliation between men. So, how do we come together? In a word—forgiveness. Forgiveness is a beautiful concept that is at the very heart of Christianity. We are a people who have been forgiven by God, and now we are called to forgive others—even when hurt deeply.

If people in the church are to have a meaningful dialogue with each other, and with those outside about the issue of racial unity, acknowledging the hurt of others and the ensuing consequences of certain acts will help create a foundation for reconciliation. Remember, Paul instructed the church to "rejoice with those who rejoice, and weep with those who weep." Engaging in meaningful discussion with others in this context provides a unique opportunity to express both biblical empathy and sympathy. In a fallen world, every relationship requires forgiveness, or else it becomes diseased. Forgiveness and godliness go hand in hand.

Joseph's Example of Forgiveness

The Context of Injustice

The Joseph narrative in Genesis 37–50 illustrates forgiveness in action. We know the story. Joseph as a teenager has a vision of the future in which his entire family bows down to him, and he reports the vision to his brothers. His brothers already have an attitude toward him, as he is their father's favorite son. Eventually, it's inflamed to the point that they plot to put him to death. Reuben intervenes, preventing his death, and hopes to rescue Joseph later. However, before Reuben returns, Joseph undergoes the heart-wrenching experience of being sold into slavery by his brothers.

Joseph is sold to a prominent official, Potiphar. Eventually, Potiphar makes him ruler of his house. But he is falsely accused by Potiphar's wife, and to save face, Potiphar puts him in prison. He eventually is put in charge of the prisoners. As you remember, at one point the baker and the butler are incarcerated with him and placed under his care. He interprets their dreams. One will be released. The other will lose his life. As they are released, as Joseph has predicted, he says to the butler, "When you come back into favor, remember me." Providentially, he forgets him, though he is restored. Joseph is forgotten and served yet another injustice at the hands of men.

The Character of Forgiveness

Finally, when Pharaoh has a mysterious dream of the famine that is coming, the butler finally remembers Joseph. Joseph is released from prison, and he interprets Pharaoh's dream. Joseph, at age thirty, is exalted to the most powerful man in Egypt apart from Pharaoh.

Now, there are seven years of plenty, and by Genesis 44, most likely, they are two or three years into the famine. So, Joseph is thirty-nine years old. At this point, his brothers come to Egypt to buy food because of the famine. Joseph recognizes his brothers, but they do not recognize him. He has had approximately twenty-two years to think about what his brothers did to him. He has had twenty-two years to say, "I will repay them when the opportunity comes." He has had twenty-two years to become bitter. He has had twenty-two years to become indifferent to, or even angry with God for allowing such a thing to happen. But he doesn't evidence any of that type of thinking. Rather, we see Joseph's character of forgiveness.

In Genesis 44, Joseph recognizes his brothers, but they don't recognize him. He tests their hearts to see if they still have no regard for the promises given to Israel (Israel being their father, but also the nation that would come from his sons).

In chapter 45, Joseph takes the initiative to reconcile with his brothers. Genesis 45:1–4 reads:

> Then Joseph could not control himself before all those who stood by him. He cried, "Make everyone go out from me." So no one stayed with him when Joseph made himself known to

his brothers. And he wept aloud, so that the Egyptians heard it, and the household of Pharaoh heard it. And Joseph said to his brothers, "I am Joseph! Is my father still alive?" But his brothers could not answer him, for they were dismayed at his presence.

So Joseph said to his brothers, "Come near to me, please." And they came near. And he said, "I am your brother, Joseph, *whom you sold into Egypt.*

That phrase "whom you sold into Egypt" is so important. It is important because Joseph still remembers what happened. It's not as if he's forgotten. Sometimes we say, "Forgive and forget." No, he remembered, perhaps very vividly, that he had been sold into slavery. He had over two decades that he could have nurtured and coddled bitterness toward them, but he didn't. He pursued reconciliation.

Notice something else about Joseph. Not only does he pursue reconciliation, but in verses 1–4 we see him *comforting his brothers.* Pause and consider his response. Such actions speak to his character. Notice verse 5: "And now do not be distressed or angry with yourselves because you sold me here." Here again, he remembers it. He knows the injustice committed. "Don't be angry because you sold me here." So he comforts those who have hurt him, displaying this desire to forgive and to be reconciled.

Not only did Joseph desire reconciliation, and not only did he comfort them, but he displayed a sense of spiritual insight and maturity as well. He had a mature understanding of God's wisdom, and God's sovereignty. Notice what he says in verses 5–8:

And now do not be distressed or angry with yourselves because you sold me here, for God sent me before you to preserve life.... And God sent me before you to preserve for you a remnant on earth, and to keep alive for you many survivors. So it was not you who sent me here, but God. He has made me a father to Pharaoh, and lord of all his house and ruler over all the land of Egypt.

Joseph possessed a perspective about life that is so necessary when it comes to forgiving other people—that God is a sovereign God, and at times he will allow hurt and difficulty in our lives.

Unfortunately, some people believe that to forgive others you need to forgive God. It is unbiblical and illogical, but some might argue that Joseph must have forgiven God for allowing all that to happen to him—and thus he was able to forgive his brothers. Rabbi Harold Kushner was popular for his seminars and a book that he authored, *When Bad Things Happen to Good People*. He toured for years espousing the view that what we have to do is learn to forgive God—we need to forgive him for creating an imperfect world. Rabbi Kushner spoke from a position of genuine personal pain, but his solution was misguided.

Some may be tempted to look at the world and say, "Okay, God, look at this imperfect world. The races are separated. There are tensions everywhere. Why did you create a world like this? I forgive you for it." This statement must be turned on its head, as men need to confess to the Lord the division they have caused by the various ways in which they have not loved their neighbors as themselves.

The Lord did not create a fallen, sin-cursed world. The Scripture is very plain that God created all things very good. It is because of our sin that we are today in need of forgiveness. But Joseph had a biblical perspective. He told his brothers: "God sent me here." And what's beautiful about it, if you go to Psalms 104–106, there's a condensed history of Israel. And in Psalm 105:17, it says that God "sent a man ahead of them, Joseph, who was sold as a slave." The psalmist would write about this episode under the inspiration of the Spirit, and declare it to be an act of God's sovereign design.

One must understand that sovereign design does not remove the consequences or human culpability for sinful actions. But having this divine perspective informs us that forgiveness can be genuinely granted to those who have sinned against us. As we will see, Joseph's brothers were still wrestling with their consciences years later. But Joseph saw a bigger picture—God's wisdom and sovereign work was being accomplished through it all.

We also notice in verses 9–15 that this perspective made Joseph generous toward others. "Hurry and go up to my father and say to him, 'Thus says your son Joseph, God has made me lord of all Egypt. Come down to me; do not tarry.'" And he goes on to say, "You shall dwell in the land of Goshen…. There I will provide for you," because there were still five years of famine to come. In verse 15, he kisses all of his brothers and weeps on them, and afterward his brothers talk with him. This reflects godly character. He was spiritually empowered because he understood God's character.

Fast-forward to Genesis 50:15. "When Joseph's brothers saw that their father was dead, they said, 'It may be that Joseph will hate us and pay us back for all the evil that we did to him.'" They're still dealing with their own guilt from what they've done. They're thinking, "Joseph is going to repay us now." "So they sent a message to Joseph, saying, 'Your father gave this command before he died: "Say to Joseph, 'Please forgive the transgression of your brothers and their sin, because they did evil to you.'" And now, please forgive the transgression of the servants of the God of your father.' Joseph wept when they spoke to him" (50:16–17).

Why would he weep? Well, he's weeping to say, "Don't you believe me? I've forgiven you. I'm free from this. I will not be bound to it." And then in verse 19, "But Joseph said to them, 'Do not fear, for am I in the place of God?'" This is so important to understand because essentially what he's saying is that for me not to forgive, I become God. In reality, there is only One who has the right to say, "I do not forgive you." When people remain unreconciled, it goes back to the core issue of a lack of forgiveness. It is spiritual pride that sits in the seat of God, the ultimate forgiver. It creates a standard that is beyond that of the Lord, which is no standard at all—it is merely a form of self-righteousness.

All of this leads to the classic statement in verse 20: "As for you, you meant evil against me, but God meant it for good, to bring it about that many people should be kept alive." We may not fully understand it all this side of glory, but even our country's participation in slavery and institutionalized racism will one day be revealed as serving a greater purpose for the good of God's people and the glory of God's Son. Does that exonerate anyone who was a part of it? No, it doesn't. But it should help us catch a glimpse of the absolute beauty of God.

You say, "Wait a minute. What do you mean? You just talked about injustices, and slavery, and institutionalized racism. How is God beautiful in that?" It comes down to a biblical theology that believes God's character revealed in the Scriptures. Experience must submit to the truth of the Scriptures. If God is beautiful, and if he's unchanging, if he is sovereign (which is how God reveals himself in the Bible), then he is that *in every circumstance in life*.

That is a comprehensive, actually an all-encompassing statement, and some may not want to accept it, but that is the biblical truth in which we find solace. Believers must embrace God's beauty and God's sovereignty by faith. I'm not promoting blind faith. But one that trusts the revelation of God's word, and his word affirms the fact of his absolute control of history. The life of Joseph is but one evidence of his sovereign beauty and wisdom.

There are times when we won't necessarily see how these difficulties and injustices resolve this side of heaven. But we believe they will, based on the evidence of the Scriptures. There is an appropriateness for all the events of history (Eccl 3:1-15; Rom 8:28). Once we embrace God's sovereign wisdom and beauty, we are prepared to embrace *forgiveness*.

Forgiveness is not just illustrated in the Scriptures, however. The Son of God himself gave us clear instructions on this radical element in reconciliation.

Jesus's Instruction on Forgiveness

Let's look at Jesus's teaching on forgiveness in Matthew 18:21: "Peter came up and said to him, 'Lord, how often will my brother sin against me, and I forgive him? As many as seven times?'" Peter likely thought his statement was magnanimous—but Jesus had a mind-blowing response. Our Lord said, "I do not say to you seven times, but seventy-seven times." Jesus elevated the standard. And he illustrated the believer's obligation to forgive with the parable of the merciful king.

He tells of a servant who owes the king and he cannot pay the debt, because verse 24 tells us that he owes the king ten thousand talents. In verse 25, he doesn't have means to repay it. What does the servant do? He prostrates himself and asks for mercy. The amount, ten thousand talents, emphasizes a point—it was impossible to pay back. And in verse 27: "And out of pity for him, the master of that servant released him and forgave him the debt." In an incredible display of folly, the forgiven slave goes out and finds a fellow slave who owes him and has him cast into prison. The other slaves hear about it and they tell the king. The king comes back and what does he say? Notice verse 32. The word order in the original is emphatic: "*All this debt* I forgave you." It's as if he is saying, "Look at the amount of debt that you were forgiven. And how dare you *not* forgive someone else." And then Jesus says in verse 34, "And in anger his master delivered him to the jailers, until he should pay all his debt."

As I mentioned earlier, ten thousand talents is a debt that cannot be repaid. So what's the point? Those who are believers in the Lord Jesus Christ are people who forgive. If you're not a person who is willing to forgive, who does not desire to forgive, I believe what it's teaching is that it reveals that you have not truly participated in genuine forgiveness. Verse 35 then teaches that if a professed believer refuses to forgive, God will put such a one in a position of having to repay a debt he can never repay. The parable implies that there is eternal separation from God if you don't forgive from the heart. Genuine believers are those who forgive because they recognize the extent of their indebtedness before God.

This message is for what audience? It's for the body of Christ. There should never be unreconciled relationships within the body of Christ. There should never be any racial divide in the church, because we have been forgiven by God and we've been made one new man. As Paul wrote in Ephesians 4:32: "Be kind to one another, tenderhearted, forgiving one another, as God in Christ forgave you." Forgiveness is necessary for any truly reconciled relationship.

If there is to be any hope of racial unity in this world, the gospel of grace must be embraced by hearts who recognize their own need for reconciliation and forgiveness before a holy God. At the heart of the gospel is the free forgiveness of sin that Christ, the King purchased at an immeasurable cost. When we grasp this by faith, our hearts are compelled by grace to forgive others who have sinned grievously against us. And where there is this type of forgiveness, there will be unity and reconciliation. Forgiveness is the radical element in racial unity. If the world is going to strive for racial unity, let it begin with those called to be lights in its midst (Phil 2:15).

EIGHT

THE LORD`S SUPPER AND RACIAL UNITY

Jim Hamilton

Not long ago, an Israeli soldier was convicted of manslaughter in Israel. A Palestinian had engaged in an attack and was subdued on the ground. As he was lying on the ground, the Israeli soldier shot him in the head. It was captured on video.

Immediately, the lines were drawn. Benjamin Netanyahu called for a pardon. Those who were partisans of Israel said that if he wasn't pardoned, the Israeli Defense organization would be crippled. The soldier's plea, his excuse, was that he didn't know whether the Palestinian on the ground had an explosive vest that he might detonate. And so he wanted to ensure that no one else was hurt. From the video, that did not appear to be much of a possibility. The parent of the Palestinian man who was slain said the Israeli soldier "should be sentenced in court like they do with the Palestinians—life sentences, torture, and then ending up dead lying in a refrigerator."

I don't bring this story up because people in our culture are any less vindictive. They aren't. I don't bring it up because people in our culture are any less deadly with weapons. They aren't. I bring it up because, as Daniel Defoe observes in his novel *Robinson Crusoe*, we can always look at other situations in our experience and recognize that things could be worse, and we can be grateful. I do think that Israeli-Palestinian racial conflicts are more complicated than the racial conflicts and tensions we're dealing with in America. Israelis and Palestinians lack gospel influence and function largely without the Word of God.

In our circumstance, we as believers are living in a culture that has been massively shaped by the Bible. Our culture is still largely influenced by the Bible, and those of us submitting to the Lord Jesus want to walk with him and be pleasing to him. Thus we have great reason for hope.

The Toxic Ingredients in the Corinthian Church

Divisions over Teachers

As we consider 1 Corinthians 11:17–34, I want us to see Paul's flow of thought leading up to that point, because what Paul does in chapter 11 is in many ways what he has done since the beginning of the letter.

From the outset, Paul has been hearing from the Corinthians via letter and in person. He has heard about the problems there in the church. And he says, "Each one of you says, 'I follow Paul,' or 'I follow Apollos,' or 'I follow Cephas,' or 'I follow Christ'" (1 Corinthians 1:12). The Christians in Corinth were identifying with particular teachers because they valued the strengths of those teachers—perhaps because they themselves had some of those same strengths.

Those saying "I follow Paul" were probably more academically inclined—people who appreciated Paul's ability to put the whole Bible together. Those who were saying "I follow Apollos" likely valued impressive speaking, and they may have been trying to be like Apollos. The Cephas contingent was perhaps made up of the doers, the people who got stuff done. And then the really spiritual people simply said, "I follow Christ."

Paul says in essence, "When I came, I did everything I could to minimize the rhetoric and celebrity effect. All I wanted you to know was Jesus, lest the cross be emptied of its power." If you're simply attracted to these things that you like and that you see in yourself, are you really getting the message of the gospel?

Thus, in the first four chapters of 1 Corinthians, Paul exposes and explodes the different divisions with the truth of the gospel.

Divisions over Sexual Issues

In chapter 5, Paul mentions a congregant who is in an illicit relationship with his father's wife. In chapter 6, church members are visiting prostitutes. And in chapter 7, some are forbidding intimacy within the context of marriage.

Notably, Paul answers these problems of sexual immorality and related issues the same way he addressed the problem of divisiveness. He writes, "Do you not know that your body is a temple of the Holy Spirit within you, whom you have from God? You are not your own, for you were bought with a price. So glorify God in your body" (1 Corinthians 6:19–20). He addresses their sexual immorality with the gospel.

Divisions over Worship Issues

In chapters 8–10, Paul addresses food offered to idols and other matters pertaining to worship. All through these chapters, Paul is redefining who these people are and how they conceive of themselves, and he's addressing their behavioral issues with the truth of the gospel. As we arrive in chapter 11, within the context worship is the antidote for idolatry, and Paul explains *how* believers need to worship the Lord.

The Table Instructions Concerning the Lord's Supper

When Worship Isn't Worship, It Makes Things Worse

So in 1 Corinthians 11:17–22, we see antigospel divisions among the Corinthians at the Lord's Supper. In 11:2, Paul says: "Now I commend you because you remember me in everything." But in 11:17 he says: "But in the following instructions I do not commend you, because when you come together it is not for the better but for the worse."

The Corinthian church thought it was coming together to worship Jesus. They thought they were coming together to honor God. And Paul says to them, "You're not making things better. You're making things worse." Then he says, "I hear that there are divisions among you" (v. 18). Again, Paul was getting reports from Corinth—and these reports were not positive. He continues: "And I believe it in part." Gordon Fee suggests that the reason he puts it this way is because he recognizes that the people giving him the reports aren't disinterested observers. Everybody has a stake, and everybody has a story. There are two sides to every story, and Paul recognizes both that there are divisions and that he's not hearing every side of the story.

Paul continues: "For there must be factions among you in order that those who are genuine among you may be recognized" (v. 19). That word "genuine" is used across the New Testament to speak of those who are approved. If you're not genuine, if you're not approved, you're not a believer. Paul is clear that this issue an issue of salvation. This is an apostle saying, "If you don't come out on the right side of my instructions here, you're not a Christian."

In verse 20 Paul says, "When you come together, it is not the Lord's supper that you eat." Every time they come together on the first day of the week they think they're partaking of the Lord's Supper, but because of the way they're practicing it, it is not the Lord's supper at all. We need hold the mirror up to ourselves. When we gather to worship, are we really worshiping God or just pleasing ourselves? Are we really remembering what Christ has done or just having a social gathering with others who share our cultural preferences?

In verse 21 Paul reveals the reason for this rebuke: "For in eating, each one goes ahead with his own meal." The wealthy—the haves—were not mindful of the have-nots. There was a lack of concern for others in the congregation. There was a self-centeredness, because culture trumped what the Lord's Supper represented.

When the Church Operates Like the Culture, Divisions Remain

The church in Corinth was operating on the norms of the wider culture. "I'm a wealthy, upper-class person. I own this place. I invite people of my class and station to dine with me at table. Meanwhile, the people that belong outside, that's where they belong." That's what's going on in Corinth. Either that, or, "Well, we're the wealthy people. We're here. We know those other people are coming, but we don't need to wait for them to get here before we start partaking."

Paul says in verse 21: "Each one goes ahead with his own meal. One goes hungry, another gets drunk." I think at verse 21, you should feel the passion of the apostle Paul. He is incensed over this. "What! Do you not have houses to eat and drink in?" (v. 22). Don't make any mistake about what he's saying here. He's saying that if you want to conduct yourself like this, then don't gather with the church. Stay home and eat like that. If you want to be a Roman, be a Roman at your house. Don't come to the church and act like that. As he says in verse 22, "Or do you despise the church of God and humiliate those who have nothing? What shall I say to you? Shall I commend you in this? No, I will not."

We should take a look in the mirror and we should ask ourselves: Why do I feel comfortable talking to certain people? What makes it so that I have easy conversations with some people and not others? Why is it so difficult to get out of my comfort zone and make somebody who's not like me feel welcome? Why do I gravitate to people who look like me, talk like me, act like me, and have what I have?

There are overt reasons why we have such difficulty answering these questions, and then there are more subtle reasons. But at root, what was wrong with the Corinthian Christians is what's wrong with us. The identity that the broader culture gives us is more prominent at a heart level, at a gut level, at an instinctual level than what the gospel says.

The Corinthians were conducting themselves as wealthy Romans who belonged to society and were living out its norms in accordance with its customs. This behavior shames the church because their identity has not been reconfigured by the gospel.

The Gospel Must Take Priority over Culture

Thus, as he has previously in this epistle, Paul attacks the Corinthian error with the Christian gospel. And he begins at verse 23 to rehearse the gospel. He's shown us in verses 17–22 these antigospel divisions in Corinth, and now he's going to tell us in verses 23–26 about the Lord's death. He says: "For I received from the Lord what I also delivered to you, that the Lord Jesus on the night when he was betrayed"—and you remember what happened on that night. The Lord Jesus had gathered together with his disciples for a Passover meal. At the Passover meal, they were commemorating the exodus from Egypt. But at that Last Supper, Jesus took this symbol of the Lord's deliverance of Israel from Egypt and in essence said to them, "This is no longer about the exodus from Egypt. This is now about my body, broken for you—the deliverance that I will accomplish through my death and resurrection."

Paul is not only recounting the way that the Lord Jesus transformed the celebration of the Passover into the celebration of his death. He is also reminding the Corinthians of the greatest self-sacrifice in history. As Paul would later write in 2 Corinthians 8:9, "You know the grace of our Lord Jesus Christ, that though he was rich, yet for your sake he became poor, so that you by his poverty might become rich."

Paul is confronting the Corinthians with the fact that they are celebrating the wealthiest, most glorious, highest one—who was broken and shamed for them—in a way that said, "I'm important. I'm significant. Look at all the money I've made. Look at all the property I have. Look at my important friends." But he says that by doing it that way they are not celebrating the Lord's Supper. Not until they're ready to say, "The greatest made himself the least. The one who is the leader made himself the servant. And in the way that I conduct myself at this table, I'm obeying his command to take up the cross and follow him."

Paul continues, rehearsing what Jesus did that night, saying, "'This is my body, which is for you. Do this in remembrance of me.' In the same way also he took the cup, after supper, saying, 'This cup is the new covenant in my blood. Do this, as often as you drink it, in remembrance of me'" (1 Corinthians 11:24–25).

Just a little side note here addressing transubstantiation, the Roman Catholic doctrine that the bread becomes the body and the wine becomes the blood: "This cup is the new covenant" parallels "This is my body" in the text. The cup does not *become* the covenant. So if the cup doesn't become the covenant, it is difficult to see how the bread becomes the body. Transubstantiation is not what Jesus intended. The cup commemorates the new covenant, and the bread commemorates the body of Christ.

Jesus is saying, "You've been commemorating the Passover all these years, the exodus from Egypt, and what I'm going to do on the cross replaces that in God's plan as this great salvific act that God has done on behalf of his people. So we're not remembering the Passover anymore. Now, you're remembering me and my death on your behalf." And the cup is a symbol of this new relationship into which God the Father brings us.

We are all one in Christ. Every tribe, tongue, language, people, background, or however else you want to classify people—the truest thing about us is not where we were born, what color our skin is, what language we grew up talking, how much money we have, how much education we have, or how many people in the culture respect us. The truest things about you and me are that we were desperate sinners and that Jesus died for us. By faith, we as believers are united to him. These are the truths we get to affirm as we partake of the Lord's Supper. "As often as you eat this bread and drink the cup, you proclaim the Lord's death until he comes" (v. 26).

Let me try to give a word of application. We need to stop making assumptions about one another. Don't assume that because I'm white I had all this access to privilege. Maybe I did. Maybe I didn't. You may not know that my eighth-grade algebra teacher told me that I would be changing tires one day.

There are all these assumptions that go around in our culture, and this is what people are saying when they say, "Don't profile me. Don't assume that because I look a certain way you know everything there is to know about me." We have to love one another enough to say, "I'm not going to make assumptions. I'm going to draw near. I'm going to ask questions. And I'm going to believe that the truest things about this person are the things I know from the gospel."

We must not trade in the secular narrative that says we display our prowess by the clothes we wear, by the jewelry we sport, by the cars we drive, by the virtues we signal, by the things we Tweet, or whatever. We reject all that, because we live in the story that says we were enslaved to sin and Christ bought us out of slavery. That's our identity. My dignity doesn't come from my achievements, or from the way that worldly people look at what I've accomplished and are impressed by it. My dignity comes from the fact that first of all I'm made in the image of God—and in Christ, God set his love on me and sent his Son to die for me. And that totally reshapes how you imagine yourself in the world.

Live in Light of Your Identity in Christ

After Paul has gone after the antigospel divisions and narrated how the Lord Jesus gave himself for the church, he moves on in verses 27–32 to tell them *how* they need to conduct themselves: "Whoever, therefore, eats the bread or drinks the cup of the Lord in an unworthy manner will be guilty concerning the body and blood of the Lord" (v. 27). What does it mean to eat and drink unworthily? I think it means not trusting in Christ. Paul seems to have in mind those whose identity hasn't been reshaped by Christ, and, as a result, maybe they're identifying with particular Christian teachers, or indulging in certain kinds of sexual immorality, or maybe they're committing various forms of idolatry, or living like a Roman and disregarding those not like themselves in the church.

It's almost like they're crucifying again the Lord of glory because they're not recognizing the value of the body of Christ. I think the reference to the body of Christ points both to his physical body and to his spiritual body, the church. Those who do not discern the body of Christ are going to be guilty concerning Jesus because they are repudiating the way he lived, giving himself for others. They will also be guilty concerning the church because they repudiate their identity with these people who believe what they profess to believe.

Verse 28 reads: "Let a person examine himself, then, and so [or in this way] eat of the bread and drink of the cup." Paul is telling the Corinthians to examine themselves. They need to look at the way they're treating other Christians, and then hold the mirror up and ask themselves, "Am I acting like Jesus here? Am I laying down my life for them?"

Paul goes on in verses 29–30: "For anyone who eats and drinks without discerning the body eats and drinks judgment on himself. That is why many of you are weak and ill, and some have died." I don't think these are Christians who have died. I think these are unbelievers whom the Lord has put to death. He then says in verses 31–32: "But if we judged ourselves truly, we would not be judged. But when we are judged by the Lord, we are disciplined so that we may not be condemned along with the world." *The Lord's Supper calls us to repent of worldliness, repent of our natural culturalism.*

"So then, my brothers, when you come together to eat, wait for [or perhaps, 'share with"] one another." It was not Roman culture to bring lower-class people into the triclinium, the room in which they dined. But Paul says that if you're a Christian, that's what you do. Verse 34: "If anyone is hungry, let him eat at home." If you don't like these instructions, Paul says, if you want to live according to your cultural appetite, then stay home. Don't gather with the church, "so that when you come together it will not be for judgment."

The Trustworthy Instructions of a Father

I don't consider myself any kind of expert on these issues. The only hope I have is in the Scriptures. And I don't pretend to say that I've never blown it on these issues. I could tell you stories about stupid things I've said and done, wicked things. So what I'm asking for is charity. I need you to be patient with me. I want to try to be patient with you. We all need the teaching of the Scriptures.

As I thought about how desperate we are for the light of God's Word, I couldn't help but think about something that happened to me when I was in seminary. I was working at a summer camp called Kanakuk down in southwestern Missouri. We worked all day long, for thirteen days straight, before getting a twenty-four-hour break. It was very taxing. So a twenty-four-hour break was like an oasis. You just can't wait for a "two-four" as they called it.

My sister worked at the same camp, and we were both scheduled for a two-four. My parents were going to come up and we were all going to go to this nearby place called Holiday Island and stay in a timeshare. But right at the time that my two-four started, I was going to have the opportunity to play in a softball game. I loved to play ball, so I wanted to stay at camp and play softball with the guys. So I said to my parents, "You guys go ahead. After the game, I'll get in my car and I'll drive to where you are."

This was July 2, 1997. We didn't have cell phones. After the game, I left camp knowing where Holiday Island was, but I didn't have a specific address. And I didn't have a phone number. At some point I realized I didn't have any idea where I was going. I had no idea how to find my mom and dad and my sister. I was lost in the world.

So I just kept driving, and eventually I saw a sign on a little building that said something like "Holiday Island timeshare rentals." I thought, "Okay, maybe I can stop here and they can tell me where to go." I stopped. It was perhaps 7:30 pm or so. Thankfully, somebody came to the door.

"Sir, my parents have rented a timeshare here on Holiday Island and I don't know which one they're in and I'm trying to find them. Can you help me?" He said, "I'm sorry, son. There are seven thousand timeshares in this area, and there is no central reservation system. I have no idea where your parents are."

Like my search for my parents at Holiday Island, we are hopeless to find our way in regard to racial unity. We have no idea where to go. We don't know where the answers are—apart from God's tender mercies and gracious instructions.

So I got in the car and started driving—not knowing really where to turn. But in his uncanny wisdom, my dad had parked my sister's car at a visible place. And as I was driving along, no idea where to go, I saw my sister's car on the side of the road. I pulled a note off the dashboard from my father telling me exactly where to go.

"Jimbo, we are at 15 Ironwood Drive on the island. Go to the island, turn right on Appaloosa Drive, second street is Ironwood Drive. Go to the end of the street, 15 Ironwood Drive. Love Dad. P.S.: it is 7:20 p.m. We will be back here at 8:20. You can stop at Island Rentals on the same street and call." I started following his instructions, and then I saw my dad coming toward me. He had the driver's-side window down, and he was hanging out the window waving at me.

Our Father is like that for us on these issues. We are in desperate need of direction. We are lost without the instructions of our Father. But he loves us, and he has given us instructions, and he will meet us. He has given us the Scriptures. Christ must be our identity—not culture. Our Father has given us a recipe for racial unity. We taste the fruit of it every time we partake of the Lord's Supper in faith—looking to Christ and caring for one another in the body of Christ.

NINE

THE FUTURE OF
RACIAL UNITY

Owen Strachan

Growing up in Maine, I was a basketball aficionado. I loved and still love basketball. And I recall what happened in my small county, Washington County, Maine, when, at one of the rival high schools, a young African American guy showed up who was clearly very talented at basketball. It caused a ripple in the whole community, in this whole county, because it was a small county, and basketball in Maine, believe it or not, is a big deal, though we produce almost no players of note.

That notwithstanding, I recall my attitude at feeling what it would be like to play in a slightly different league and recognizing that this player was going to be a new challenge. He talked a certain way. He had a kind of culture that he brought with him from Texas. It was a really cool opportunity for me and many others to get acquainted with someone from another culture, another ethnic or racial background.

There was a sense even of excitement and wonder in that. That is not the way many people in America feel today on the topic of race. *Wonder*— we would not always use that word. Perhaps we would not even think to use the term *wonder* at the fact that there are so many races and ethnicities, for example, throughout America.

Today, in order to understand race and eschatology in proper biblical perspective, we need to recover this very vocabulary. *We need to recover a sense of the beauty of racial diversity, ethnic diversity,* not simply in our society, of course, but also in God's local church.

Protology

If you want to understand eschatology, where things are going, where things terminate, you need to understand *protology,* where things begin, the original design of God for his creation.

Created for God—Not Division

We know from Genesis 1–2 that God did not create humanity for division. There is nothing embedded in a prefall creation that would lead us to think that race or ethnicity should be a problem for us. There's *nothing,* in fact, in the original creation that is supposed to be a problem for us.

Humanity derives its existence and ongoing life from the mind and the hand of God. And God's design for mankind involved worship—not self-worship, but Creator worship. In the early chapters of Genesis, the primary way to worship God is to obey God. This is the Christian worldview. This is the biblical perspective—unlike what our culture teaches. According to Genesis 1–2, God did not create by any kind of scientific process that can only be known thousands of years later to humanity. God used his own ingenuity and his own hand to make mankind. Many of us take this for granted and overlook the tremendous theological import in these early chapters. We need to take note of its significance in the matter of humanity.

The ground of man's unity is established in Genesis 1–2.

The Scriptures know nothing of some primordial amoebic origin. The ground of our unity is the fact that we are made by God—and he made us for himself. That's how humanity is initially united. He made the man and the woman out of his super-intelligence to display his superior glory. We are not cosmic accidents. You and I are here because God made a man and a woman, and the human race proliferated over the ages. God made this race specially for himself.

Created an Enchanted Race

The cosmos is teeming with diversity. Anytime you watch one of those National Geographic specials you hear about the wonders of nature and the wonders of creation. But the majestic scenery, the exotic plants, or any part of the animal kingdom you want to name is not made as humanity is made—to uniquely display the glory of God. We are an enchanted race. Our origin makes it so.

I'm writing a book called *Re-enchanting Humanity*, and it's supposed to be a biblical anthropology covering these kinds of themes. In the last two or three centuries of intellectual history we've become a race that has lost its glory. The implications of evolutionary theory have led us to the practical conclusion that there's nothing unique about us. We're just like the apes, we're told. But God's Word clearly reveals that we are an enchanted race—specially formed by God from the beginning to uniquely display his glory. The man and the woman are created as vice regents of creation underneath the sovereignty of God. They are made to have dominion over every beast, everything in the world including the creeping thing.

The Created Order Upended

Sadly, there was a real historical fall of Adam and Eve. In Genesis 3:1–13, the created order is upended.

The serpent upends the order and approaches the woman. The woman leads her husband—not the creational order God intended—and they fall. They eat the forbidden fruit. Every bad thing in this world traces its origins back to that event. If every evil thing gloriously comes untrue in the kingdom of Jesus Christ by the power of his cross, every bad thing comes true in the fall of Adam.

Adam is the head of the human race. He represents all of us. He was called to have leadership over us, over his home, over his family. Thus every bad thing that you and I experience traces back to Genesis 3. As believers, we understand why there is sin, turmoil, hatred, disunity, lack of peace in our home, in our neighborhood, in our city or town or suburb, and certainly in our world. The early chapters of Genesis show us why the world is the way it is. Only believers, those who make up the true church, know why things are the way they are.

If you don't know the beginning, you will not know the end. If you don't know the beginning, you will not know how to solve the problem. If we are going have an answer for such a tremendous problem as racial disunity, as racism, we are going to need to know the origins of that problem. Only Scripture has the answers.

United in Opposition to God

In Genesis 10, the sons of Noah were established as the first of numerous people groups. There was just one language among all the peoples of the earth. But instead of spreading to fill the earth after the flood, as God commanded, once again humanity set itself against the gracious authority of its Creator. Note Genesis 11:4–9:

> Then they said, "Come, let us build ourselves a city and a tower with its top in the heavens, and let us make a name for ourselves, lest we be dispersed over the face of the whole earth." And the LORD came down to see the city and the tower, which the children of man had built. And the LORD said, "Behold, they are one people, and they have all one language, and this is only the beginning of what they will do. And nothing that they propose to do will now be impossible for them. Come, let us go down and there confuse their language, so that they may not understand one another's speech." So the LORD dispersed them from there over the face of all the earth, and they left off building the city. Therefore its name was called Babel, because there the Lord confused the language of all the earth. And from there the Lord dispersed them over the face of all the earth.

The peoples actually were united in Genesis 11. They had a common goal. They wanted to build a city and a tower, and they want to make a name for themselves. Just as ethnicity and race emerged in human experience, there was initial unity.

Did it redound to the praise and glory of Almighty God? No. The various ethnicities were unified, but their unity did not include any mention of the honor and glory of God. Rather they were unified in their opposition to the revealed will of God. In Genesis 1:26–28, God gave mankind a prefall mandate to fill the earth and subdue it. The command to fill the earth was repeated after the flood—to Noah and his sons. All the peoples were to fill the earth under God's gracious blessing.

But Genesis 11:4 says: "Let us make a name for ourselves, lest we be dispersed over the face of the whole earth." They were rejecting the original plan of God for the entire human race.

In a fallen world, the peoples do not see either unity or diversity as a means to glorify God. They should yearn to image God's glory, even as they have become separate tribes and peoples (Genesis 10). But from the introduction of diversity in a postfall world, the opposite occurs.

We have not been God-oriented in terms of our background, in terms of our core humanity, in terms of our diversity, ethnicity, race—choose your marker—since the fall. Humanity has been messed up profoundly in racial and ethnic terms from just about the start of the whole story following Genesis 3.

United in Seeking Dominion over One Another

Very soon after Genesis 11, peoples began going to war against one another. They started hunting each other down and killing each other for no—really, honestly—no good reason.

That phrase "for no good reason" applies to so much of our humanity. I think about some of what occurs in a household with a five-year-old and a two-year-old in particular. And I did this too when I was a kid, because I'm a sinner in Adam just as everyone else is in Adam. But there are things that take place—here's this phrase again—for no good reason. There are feelings that are hurt, seriously for no purpose. There's no end that is being served. Destruction takes place of various Lego-driven facilities in my home, and there's no good reason for it. There's not a greater purpose. It's not that the two-year-old girl has dreamed up a greater Lego facility and her vision must logically supersede that of her five-year-old brother.

No, there's just hostility for hostility's sake. And it didn't originate in the Strachan household. It goes all the way back. The peoples of the earth as we see in these chapters in Genesis seek dominion not over the earth as they are called to have; they seek dominion over one another.

We still are going to war against one another. It may not be in the streets, though sometimes it is. Sometimes it's simply in the quietness of our thoughts. It may be on private email, or text threads that nobody sees but our closest friends. It is in the heart of man to go to war against man. It is in the heart of man further to use our markers, our natural differences, as those lines that determine who we are going to war against.

In Adam, we do not see our bodies and lives as vessels of praise to God. Instead, in Adam, we see our bodies and our lives as vehicles of self-expression on the one hand and domination on the other. Neither of those motives is natural to Adam and Eve before the fall.

We're in a ruined world. This world has been shot through with sin, and the human race is in tatters because of it. This leads us to my second point.

Eschatology

In spite of all the evil with us in this fallen world, there remains unmistakable grandeur. Look around with you with your eyes open and you cannot help but see intoxicating beauty. The Christian is redeemed, and given eyes to see the beauty of what God has done, and in some measure is doing.

But even as we gaze on the work of God that yet beckons our attention in this world, we know that this world is hostile. In Titus 3:1–3, Paul writes, "Remind them to be submissive to rulers and authorities, to be obedient, to be ready for every good work, to speak evil of no one, to avoid quarreling, to be gentle, and to show perfect courtesy toward all people. For we ourselves were once foolish, disobedient, led astray, slaves to various passions and pleasures, passing our days in malice and envy, *hated by others and hating one another.*"

We exist primarily in a culture of hatred. We, in our flesh, eagerly, naturally participate in it. We're very glad to. We're very glad to hate others, and we're even ready to be hated by others. Again, we are primed for war. This isn't what God intended for us, but this is where we find ourselves.

A New Kingdom—Inaugurated in the Blood of Christ

The Christian gospel, however, which comes in the name and the work of Jesus Christ, means that there's something better than this hate-filled, divisive, fallen order. In Christ, the age to come has broken into the present age. Mark 1:14–15: "Now after John was arrested, Jesus came into Galilee, proclaiming the gospel of the kingdom of God, and saying, 'The time is fulfilled, and the kingdom of God is at hand; repent and believe in the gospel.'"

Sometimes I wonder if we as believers have missed the sentence, "The kingdom of God is at hand." Because of the person and work of Jesus Christ, the age to come has broken into our world. Heaven has broken into earth.

With the incarnation and earthly ministry of Jesus, in some senses, he has inaugurated the kingdom. He brought the message of it when he began his public ministry as you see in Mark 1. And in his death on the cross, he cut a new covenant and he inaugurated in blood a new kingdom. Jesus laid claim to his people. Jesus secured the salvation of his people. Jesus created, you could say, by his cross work, a new kingdom, a new political order, a new country essentially, in which believers find their citizenship.

All of this means that every believer, everyone who trusts in Jesus as their Savior, is a citizen of heaven, and now lives willingly under the rule of God—and is able to live out a new ethic. We're able to transcend the hatred of others, which is naturally in our heart as well. We're able to rise above this world. We are able to be submissive and gentle (Titus 3). We're able, by the Spirit's power, to overcome our natural desires and instincts (Galatians 5:16–24).

Reflecting Heaven—Reflect on Heaven

The apostolic plan for us to live according to a new kingdom ethic is found in one place: the local church. The local church is the sign of the kingdom. The local church is a little outpost of heaven in a world of lies. Every gospel-preaching, Jesus-loving, local church is a word of grace to sinners, and a word of judgment to the wicked.

The local church is all about the love of Jesus Christ. But the local church also is a foretaste, a sign to the world that all is not right with the world. So part of what our local churches have to do and to be is to make good on the kingdom vision of Jesus and his apostles—and show people a little picture of the new heavens and new earth.

The people who most compel others to come and see what Jesus is about are those who think deeply, longingly, meditatively about God and about the end of all things, the new heavens and the new earth.

This fallen world is desperate to convince you not to think about heaven, and especially not to think about the God of heaven. But as a believer, there is nothing you could do that would be of greater value than to think about your God and to think about the end of all things that he is preparing for his church—for his bride.

Any second, any moment you spend treasuring up God, is a moment infinitely well spent, a moment snatched from the claws of Satan. Satan would have you lose yourself in this world. Satan would have you get lost in anger, and frustration, and anxiety. This tactic of the enemy is alive and well in race relations, politics, personal relationship, and a host of other areas. The spirit of the age is to lose yourself in anything and everything other than Jesus Christ and the glory to come.

Social media, the news, conversations with unbelievers all tempt us to spend all day focusing on crises and controversies. But God's Word calls us to set our minds on things above (Colossians 3:1–4). Consider, therefore, John's vision of the new heavens and the new earth in Revelation 21:22–27:

> And I saw no temple in the city, for its temple is the Lord God the Almighty and the Lamb. And the city has no need of sun or moon to shine on it, for the glory of God gives it light, and its lamp is the Lamb. By its light will the nations walk, and the kings of the earth will bring their glory into it, and its gates will never be shut by day—and there will be no night there. They will bring into it the glory and the honor of the nations. But nothing unclean will ever enter it, nor anyone who does what is detestable or false, but only those who are written in the Lamb's book of life.

This is more real than the latest social media hot take. This passage in Revelation 21 is more sure than anything any political strategist on any side cooks up. The most practical thing in the world for you and me to do is to meditate on this vision. This is where things are headed. Not far off, soon and very soon, we will all be *one* in heaven—a wondrously enchanted race of diverse people unified in the worship of God. There will be no dividing lines in the city whose light is Christ.

Knowing the future means we can experience transformation in the present. Our very real eschatological unity is the best means anyone could ever offer you for beginning to work toward racial unity. But we have to remember that the ground of this unity is not positive feelings. It's Jesus Christ. The summing up of all things in Jesus Christ is where things are going.

That's really what eschatology has to offer the church. That's what the book of Revelation is teaching the church. There are tough texts that all folks on different sides have to handle, but Jesus Christ, we can agree, at the end of Revelation is where this is headed and where this is realized.

Revelation 21:23 again: "And the city has no need of sun or moon to shine on it, for the glory of God gives it light, and its lamp is the Lamb." People like to ask, "What is heaven going to be like? Are we going to play soccer there? Is there going to be coffee and football and Parcheesi in the new heavens and the new earth?" I don't know. I don't exactly know what the new heavens and new earth looks like, or will be like, but I know this, heaven is not boring. Heaven for the Christian is all about Jesus Christ.

If Jesus is your treasure now, heaven will be glorious. There won't be anything boring about it.

I don't know whether there will be the finest roasted dark coffee you've ever tasted in your life. Maybe there will be in the new heavens and new earth. I don't know. What I do know is that the kings of the earth stream into the city of God, the realized city, the new heavens and new earth. And the Lamb is their light.

Outside of Jesus, you can have temporary peace and temporary unity. And I am not down on temporary peace and unity. I'm glad that America is not engaged in World War III at present. But I have to have things in proper eschatological, theological, biblical perspective. I have to know that no matter what you and I cook up for social solutions, we are not Jesus.

How much good would it do the public square if people would recognize this. And if people, instead of just merely recognizing this, would then turn to Jesus as the source for what ails us, for the unity that Christ creates is so strong that nothing can break it. The very power of God is behind Christian unity. There is nothing stronger in this world. There is no ethnic community, united as it may be, that can match the unity afforded us in the gospel of Jesus Christ.

We are not waiting for a solution to our racial struggles. We're not waiting for someone to propose it. It is here. Jesus Christ has broken into this age. Jesus Christ has inaugurated a kingdom in his blood that brings sinners of every type and kind together.

Genuine and lasting racial unity is eschatological. It's grounded in knowing where things are headed, and being one family in the new heavens and the new earth. Racial unity is christological. It's grounded in Jesus Christ, who alone can make one new man. Perhaps not perfectly, but genuinely, believers here and now can overcome ethnic and racial differences—because we have a higher allegiance, higher calling, and unified vision grounded in the new heavens and new earth.

Practical Takeaways

1. Be a Christian who meditates regularly on heaven. Think more about heaven than you do. Have a goal, by the Spirit's power, of thinking more about God than anything in this world. If you want a guide to this, I've written some books on Jonathan Edwards. Jonathan Edwards was not a perfect man, but he was a God-intoxicated man.

2. When you see reports of racial violence, grieve. We know why things go wrong here. Christians must never be coldhearted to human suffering wherever it is found. But also, as you grieve, allow yourself to be refreshed by the truth that soon Jesus will come back in glory and will conquer the world. This will save you from the despair and

anxiety and unending frustration that is all around us in every ethnic community today.

3. Remember that the kings of the earth come to worship Christ in Revelation 21. This is telling us that now, as in the new heavens and new earth, Christ is our all. There's not another solution for the cure of sin besides Jesus in this world. There's one solution. God has offered it in Christ.

4. Take time to learn who other people are. American evangelicalism believes in "zap it" evangelism. Basically, you get in and get out as quickly as you can. You share that gospel in thirty seconds flat. It's like the world's fastest tire change.

   But I would say in moments like this, when we are racially fractured as a society and culture, at least part of the solution to what ails us is taking time to listen to other people, to learn what their background is, to hear them out—not for data gathering—but as a human being, a fellow image bearer.

   Does it ever startle you to learn who people actually are, and the uniqueness of their background? This is part of the wonder of being made in the image and likeness of God as human beings. You find out fascinating things about people who look very ordinary. And this is true along racial lines. People surprise you.

   Our society is training us to size people up in a second, and judge them, and cut them off. We have to stop falling prey to the kind of divisions that our secular, God-denying culture loves. We have to do the hard work of learning who our neighbor is.

5. Work constantly for racial unity wherever you can— whenever you can. Not just through sharing the gospel. Through befriending somebody in your community,

encounters at Starbucks, wherever you are, in your workplace—do the small things. You and I, most of us, can't pull the levers to change American society. A few people can and a few people have in American history. They have done tremendous things to make this society more equitable. And we are thankful for that. But most of us can't do that. We think we can through our Twitter account. We can't.

Here's what we can do: we can work for on-the-ground racial unity, which, by the way, is often more lasting and more consequential. Beware of practicing your righteousness on Twitter.

Finally, remember this. The church of the Lord Jesus Christ is a foretaste of the age to come. The church is a little sign of heaven now, the new heavens and new earth. The church is the place where hostility goes to die. The church is the place where people are friends, more than friends, brothers and sisters, for no reason other than Jesus Christ. When a church is operating in that kind of dynamic, then yes, it is truly reflecting the glories of heaven to a lost and dying world.

The future promises a racially diverse, yet gloriously unified humanity worshiping Christ. We must keep this in front of us at all times as we relate to one another in church and in the world. If we do, we will reveal God's final word on racial unity.

TEN

THE MINISTRY OF SPURGEON AND RACIAL UNITY

Christian George

To me, though I am the very least of all the saints, this grace was given, to preach to the Gentiles the unsearchable riches of Christ, and to bring to light for everyone what is the plan of the mystery hidden for ages in God, who created all things, so that through the church the manifold wisdom of God might now be made known to the rulers and authorities in the heavenly places. This was according to the eternal purpose that he has realized in Christ Jesus our Lord, in whom we have boldness and access with confidence through our faith in him. So I ask you not to lose heart over what I am suffering for you, which is your glory. (Ephesians 3:8–13)

At six in the evening on Thursday, December 1, 1955, Rosa Parks refused to give up her seat to a white passenger on the city bus in Montgomery, Alabama. Parks was arrested for disobeying Chapter 6, Section 11 of the Segregation Law of Alabama requiring all black people to relinquish their seats to whites when a bus reached its maximum capacity. Parks's act of civil disobedience became a symbol of courage and hope. It became a symbol of optimism for the civil rights movement in the 1950s and 1960s. And she emboldened others like Martin Luther King Jr. to stand up for the rights of those who had very few.

But if you had been alive ninety-five years earlier, on February 17, 1860, you would have seen another manifestation of racial injustice in that same square. In Montgomery, a bonfire was blazing not far from the jail where Parks would later be imprisoned. And if you were standing close enough to that bonfire, you would have seen the sermons of Charles Haddon Spurgeon being thrown into the flames.

A week earlier, a newspaper had issued the following call to action: "A gentleman of this city requests us to invite, and we hereby invite all persons in Montgomery who possess copies of the sermons of the notorious English abolitionist, Spurgeon—to send them to the jail yard to be burned on next Friday. A subscription is also on foot to buy of our booksellers all copies of said sermons now in their stores to be burnt on the same occasion."

A follow-up article was published later that week. It said this: "Last Saturday, we devoted to the flames a large number of copies of Spurgeon's sermons. We trust that the works of this greasy, cockney vociferator may receive the same treatment throughout the South. And if the pharisaical author should ever show himself in these parts, we trust that a stout cord may find its way speedily around his eloquent throat."

On March 22 of that year, a "Vigilance Committee" burned Spurgeon's sermons in that square. A week later, Mr. Davis, a bookstore owner on Market Street in Montgomery, prepared a good fire of pine sticks before reducing sixty volumes of Spurgeon's sermons to "smoke and ashes." Throughout the Southern states, bonfires illuminated jail yards and plantations and bookstores and courthouses. Churches would often have a potluck dinner on Wednesday night before meeting to burn Spurgeon's sermons afterward.

In Virginia, a Baptist preacher by the name of Mr. Kuber, who was a highly respected citizen, burned seven calf-skinned volumes of Spurgeon's sermons on the head of a flower barrel. In North Carolina, Spurgeon's very famous sermon "Turn or Burn" found a similar fate when a man by the name of Mr. Punch turned to the second page and then burned the whole thing.

It was said in 1860 that slave-owning pastors throughout the South were foaming with rage because they could not lay their hands on this youthful, "hypocritical" preacher. In Florida, Spurgeon was called a "beef-eating, puffed-up, vain, over-righteous, pharisaical, English blab mouth." In Virginia, he was said to be a "fat, over-grown boy." Now, Spurgeon was five foot five and three hundred pounds.

In Louisiana, he was called a "hell-deserving Englishman." In South Carolina, he was called a "vulgar, young man with soiled, slick hair and a self-satisfied air." Georgians were encouraged to pay no attention to Spurgeon. North Carolinians wanted to murder Spurgeon. They called him a hypocrite. Any bookseller in Raleigh who owned copies of Spurgeon's sermons was immediately arrested and charged with circulating incendiary publications.

The Southern Baptist denomination ranked among Spurgeon's chief antagonists. The *Mississippi Baptist* newspaper hoped that "no Southern Baptist will now purchase any of Spurgeon's books." The Baptist colporteurs of Virginia were forced by law to return all of his sermons to the publisher.

What did this twenty-six-year-old preacher in London do to elicit so fiery and hateful a reaction?

Before answering that question, we need some introduction to the man himself. He was a man who sacrificed his reputation, his friendships, his finances, and nearly his very life to defend the rights of enslaved men and women throughout the United States.

It is my hope that you will walk away after reading this chapter admiring not only Spurgeon himself but, much more so, Spurgeon's Savior.

The Life and Times of Spurgeon

A Changing World

Charles Spurgeon was born in 1834, only ten days after the famous Baptist missionary William Carey passed away. The white-hot fervor of George Whitefield and Jonathan Edwards had begun to cool in England. A new day had dawned for the empire on which the sun never set.

It dawned theologically, and it also dawned technologically. Spurgeon was born into a world of upgrade on the one hand, and downgrade on the other hand. Over the course of his life, light bulbs replaced gas lamps, engines replaced animals, and gear-driven gadgets and inventions of all kinds made life easier than previous generations.

William Carey was given a thirty-year life expectancy. For Andrew Fuller and the next generation, that number rose only by four. Spurgeon's generation only expected forty years of life when he was born in 1834.

His was the age of rubber bands and safety pins. We take those for granted. Sewing machines could stitch an astonishing one thousand yards of fabric every day. Lawnmowers absolutely revolutionized agriculture. In Spurgeon's day, photography, still an industry in infancy, began to capture history as it happened.

Progress became the quintessential Victorian virtue. The first postage stamp entered circulation when Spurgeon was only five years old. The word *dinosaur* was coined around his eighth birthday. At eleven, Spurgeon could walk on pavement instead of cobblestone. And as a teenager, he might have even flushed the world's first public toilet at the Great Exhibition in 1851, which he attended in June of that year.

An Influential Ministry

Spurgeon was twenty-one years old when the first biography was written about his life. By the end of 1857, both sides of the Atlantic knew his name. A young child in Chicago was asked by his schoolteacher, "Who is the prime minister of England?" He answered, "Well, of course, it is Charles Spurgeon."

By the end of the decade, Spurgeon had become the most popular preacher in the world. His voice could reach audiences of 3,000 or even 23,000. There were 23,654 people in attendance at the Crystal Palace one day when Spurgeon was preaching. The newspapers interviewed a child and asked, "Can you hear the preacher preach? He was just a dot in the distance." (Some estimate Spurgeon was nearly a mile away.) The child answered: "It sounded like the preacher was sitting right next to me whispering in my ear."

Today, we know Spurgeon not because we hear him preach on the internet, radio, or television. We know Spurgeon from his printed sermons. His sermons were published every week. They were translated into forty languages, and they eventually totaled sixty-three volumes.

D. L. Moody once commented, "It is a sight in Colorado on Sunday to see the miners come out of the bowels of the hills and gather at school houses under the trees while some old English miner stands up and reads one of Charles Spurgeon's sermons."

In 1884, a Christian in China wrote Spurgeon a letter and said he'd rather miss a meal than miss Spurgeon's spiritual food. In January of 1883 a murderer awaiting execution in Brazil was last seen reading a Spurgeon sermon just before he was hanged.

In Australia, a convict escaped from prison. He Shawshanked his way out of there. He murdered somebody in cold blood with a knife, looted the pockets of his victim, and what did he find but a bloodstained sermon by Charles Spurgeon. Right then and right there, he was converted to the Christian faith. Even owning Spurgeon's sermons is evangelistic regardless of whether you're alive!

By the end of his life, Spurgeon published more words in the English language than any preacher in the history of the church.

A Controversial Ministry

But Spurgeon also lived in an age of downgrade. The church of Spurgeon's day sparked as much with controversy and crisis as it did with electricity. There was a crisis of doubt unraveling around him. Did Jesus really rise from the grave? Is Jesus really God? Can science and faith somehow find a way to coexist together?

By the end of his life, in 1892, Spurgeon withdrew his membership from the Baptists of his day, and he did this because he could not in good conscience remain in fellowship with those who denied the key tenets of Scripture. Namely, that the Word of God is infallible and that Jesus Christ is really God.

Now for some people like Mark Twain, who visited Spurgeon's Tabernacle in 1879, Spurgeon's theology looked like a fossil from a previous era. Twain was going to see Charles Darwin, but before he did, he wrote in his diary, "I went over to the Tabernacle and heard Mr. Spurgeon. The sermon was three-fourths of an hour long. The topic was treated in an unpleasant, old fashion." He also said he hated the weather that day so he was not in a good mood.

But to others, like Florence Nightingale, and Lottie Moon, and Hudson Taylor, and also the twentieth president of the United States, James Garfield, Spurgeon was a symbol of light and life. Garfield visited the Tabernacle in 1867 and in his diary wrote, "God bless Mr. Spurgeon. He is helping to work out the problem of religious and civil freedom for England."

A Partner in Ministry

Though perhaps not overwhelmed by Spurgeon at first, his wife Susannah was by his side through much of his ministry. When she first laid eyes on him in 1854, she didn't think much about him. Charles was from the country. He had a thick accent. Susannah said it sounded more like a deformity than a dialect.

Susannah was a city girl. This is how she described him: "What a painful countrified manner he has, and his hair, why it looks like he's a barber's assistant." Even still, the two fell in love and were married. Susannah basically cleaned Spurgeon up. She took away the polka-dotted handkerchief he would always annoyingly wave in the pulpit. I think she threw it away.

But they didn't have an easy life. In 1865, Susannah underwent a botched surgery that rendered her infertile for the rest of her life. She was bedridden for fifteen years. Charles took care of her. Charles himself had health problems, and often found himself oscillating between depression and illness, between gout on the one hand and doubt on the other hand.

But they were a team. They were a team in marriage. They were a team in ministry. On one occasion, Spurgeon forgot to do his sermon prep. In the middle of the night, Susannah heard somebody talking. It was her husband preaching a sermon, apparently in his sleep. And what did Susannah do? Well, probably most wives would put a pillow over their head, or maybe over his head, but she took a pen and paper and started writing down everything he was saying in his sleep.

The next morning, Spurgeon woke up. He was in a panic. "I forgot to do my sermon prep." And his wife handed him her notes. And guess what—he preached from those notes. We have that sermon. It's quite good.

Spurgeon's Abolitionist Convictions

But where did Spurgeon's journey to faith begin? And more to the point, where did the source of his abolitionist convictions originate? Well, it began in a primitive Methodist chapel in Colchester, England, on January 6 or possibly 13, 1850. The fifteen-year-old was trying to make his way to another church when he got lost in a violent snowstorm. It was a blizzard. Meteorological accounts of that day said it wiped out the whole city. Everything was at a standstill.

Spurgeon stumbled into this little church soaking wet and weary. The pastor was snowed in. There was only a handful of people in the room. And suddenly, right as it looked like the service was going to be over, a shoemaker or a tailor, a man Spurgeon never met again in his life, climbed up into the pulpit and began preaching a sermon on Isaiah 45:22, "Look unto Me and be ye saved all the ends of the earth." Spurgeon said it was the worst sermon he had ever heard.

The preacher seemed to struggle to know what to say in regard to Isaiah 45:22. And so he was forced to repeat his text over and over and over again. Spurgeon said it was delivered in the worst accent he's ever heard. But the text was repeated: "Look unto Me and be ye saved." "Look unto Me and be ye saved."

In the middle of this sermon, this man pointed his finger down at young Charles from the pulpit and said this: "Young man, you look very miserable and you will always be miserable. You'll be miserable in life and you'll be miserable in death unless you obey the words of my text. 'Look unto Me and be ye saved all the ends of the earth.'"

Spurgeon later reflected, "I looked to Christ that day as though I could have looked my eyes away." This story reminds us that you don't have to be a Spurgeon for God to use you to convert a Spurgeon.

We don't necessarily need any more famous Christians. We need more faithful Christians. Because of the faithful obedience of that humble stranger, ten million people would hear the gospel of Jesus Christ by the end of the nineteenth century.

After Spurgeon's conversion, he decided to become a Baptist. He did not return to that Methodist church. His mother was shocked. "Ah, Charles," she said, "I often prayed the Lord to make you a Christian, but I never asked that you might become a Baptist." To which Spurgeon said, "Ah, mother, the Lord has answered your prayer with His usual bounty and has given you exceedingly, abundantly more and above all that you could have asked or thought."

After his conversion to Christ, Spurgeon's heart began to soften. Racial unity doesn't come naturally to us. Sin is the root of racism. Unity didn't come naturally for Spurgeon, and it won't come naturally for you and for me. God must tenderize us.

God had to emancipate Spurgeon's heart before he could help others find their freedom. "There is another slavery," said Spurgeon, "a slavery into which all of us are born. A slavery in which we have lived, and alas, a slavery under which some of us still live. But Jesus Christ has come, the Great Liberator to proclaim liberty to the captives."

For the first time in his life, Spurgeon's heart was opened in that snowstorm, not only to Jesus Christ but also to the victimized and the disenfranchised of his day. A few months after that morning, Spurgeon recorded his financial expenditures of the week. We can see how he spent his money that year. He bought books. He bought letters. And yet, there was something different in his expense ledger. He was also giving money to the poor—the shoe boy, the woman who kept her shop open on Sunday, the poor black man.

Spurgeon's stance against racial injustice would certainly become more than the giving of his resources, but it was not less. If you really want to see the character of a man, look at how he spends his money. Here, we can trace the first few seeds of what would later blossom into a life committed to combating injustice wherever Spurgeon discovered it.

In the Spurgeon library, we have about fifteen researchers and we're interested in all facets of Charles Spurgeon, all sorts of things. One thing that we recently discovered is how much Spurgeon was worth. From 1870 to 1891, Spurgeon earned the equivalent of 26 million dollars. In his more productive years, he probably quadrupled if not more of that. We think he may have been worth somewhere around 100 million dollars over the course of his life.

In New York City, his sermons were selling a thousand copies a minute at trade shows. And yet, at the end of his life, Charles Spurgeon died relatively poor. He only died with two thousand pounds in his bank account. Why? Spurgeon gave all of his money away—not just the interest of his money. He gave the principal.

He funneled all his resources into sixty-six ministries in London. Many of those he personally financed for his whole life. He started a Sunday school for the blind. He started a book fund with his wife. Nursing homes. Nobody in his day demonstrated more love for the least of these than Charles Spurgeon.

Spurgeon believed that each human being is made in the image of God. Inspired by his friend George Müller, he founded two orphanages that provided for 500 boys and 500 girls. He started a ministry for prostitutes, or fallen women, as they were called back then. In 1857, there were 8,600 prostitutes in his ministerial district.

Spurgeon's passion to help the oppressed extended to the issue of slavery. Nowhere is his detestation of slavery more pronounced than in his friendship with Thomas L. Johnson. Johnson was a slave from Virginia. He later wrote a memoir called *28 Years a Slave*. He first heard about Spurgeon from his slave masters. They were criticizing and making fun of the abolitionist preacher from England.

After Johnson was emancipated in 1865, he traveled to Denver, Colorado, and he read a pamphlet by Spurgeon called *The Preacher's Prayers*. The former slave said, "No book that I possessed at that time apart from Scripture gave me such assistance." Johnson traveled to London to meet with Spurgeon. He enrolled as a student at The Pastors' College, and he was so nervous about meeting Spurgeon that when he first arrived he was shaking. Until, that is, he actually met Spurgeon. He said it was like meeting an old friend. Spurgeon personally discipled Thomas, and he commissioned him as a missionary to Africa. For the rest of his life, Spurgeon paid all his expenses.

In Ephesians 3:10 Paul tells us that he was given the gospel "so that through the church the manifold wisdom of God might now be made known to the rulers and authorities in the heavenly places." The manifold wisdom of God—*polypoikilos*, multicolorful. The root of the term translated "manifold wisdom" was used in the Greek Old Testament, which is called the Septuagint, to describe Joseph's multicolored robe (see Genesis 37:3). God never intended a monochrome Christianity. Racial unity is not about sameness. It's about oneness. Jesus wasn't crossing his fingers in John 17:21 when he prayed "that they may all be one, just as you, Father, are in me, and I in you." And like that multicolored robe that Joseph's brothers covered with the blood of an animal, you and I are one if we are covered in the blood of the Lamb.

On July 6, 1887, Frederick Douglass wrote Spurgeon a letter. This is what he said: "Dear Mr. Spurgeon, while crossing the Atlantic last September and looking out upon its proud dashing billows and their varied forms and thinking about the diversity in the human family, I remarked that we are many as the waves, but we are one as the sea." That was a reminder for Spurgeon.

One year before Spurgeon was born, the hard work of William Wilberforce had succeeded in passing the Slavery Abolishment Act of 1833. So you could say Spurgeon was really a first-generation abolitionist to continue Wilberforce's work. And because of this, half a million of his sermons, probably more, were destroyed throughout the Southern states.

Spurgeon was vocal about the evils of slavery in his time. He called it "man stealing." He believed it was a sin worth breaking fellowship over. "I do from my inmost soul detest slavery anywhere and everywhere, although I commune at the Lord's Table with men of all creeds. Yet, with a slaveholder, I have no fellowship of any sort for any kind."

In 1859, an American minister by the name of Reverend H.—we don't know the rest of his name, but he traveled from Mobile, Alabama, to London to meet the young Charles Spurgeon. Spurgeon was planning on coming to America to raise money in 1861 for his tabernacle. When he asked this Alabamian if it was wise to come, the man from Alabama discouraged it for the reason that Charles Spurgeon would have surely been executed. In doing so, I think this no-name pastor from Alabama saved Spurgeon's life.

In 1859, Charles Darwin published *On the Origin of Species*. People started believing the earth was more than a few thousand years old. There was a crisis of faith brewing among the Victorians. And when Spurgeon openly criticized the theory of evolution in his 1861 lecture, the newspapers crucified him. "We are now to be entertained by Mr. Spurgeon's lecture on the gorilla but in after ages, we shall doubtless have a gorilla lecturing on Mr. Spurgeon." Other newspapers portrayed him as being arrogant and bigheaded, as a lion of London who growled out a vulgar gospel.

Spurgeon did his best to maintain a good attitude. I like what he says: "Don't get upset when people speak poorly of you. You are far worse than they could ever know." In 1887, the people in Spurgeon's life began to speak very poorly of the preacher. In the same year that Lottie Moon requested her Christmas offering from China, Spurgeon wrote his own letter lamenting the theological climate of his day: "The atonement is scouted. The inspiration of Scripture is derided. The Holy Ghost is downgraded. The punishment of sin has turned into a fiction and the resurrection into a myth." He was a preacher who would not compromise on his conviction that only when Jesus Christ is at the very center of your life can your life ever be truly centered.

In January of 1888, Spurgeon withdrew his membership from the Baptist Union. His own brother James, along with eighty of his students from the college, turned their backs on Charles. It put the preacher into such a state of despondency that, according to his wife, the controversy led to his premature death at the age of fifty-seven.

At 11:05 p.m. on January 31, 1892, Spurgeon passed away. Thanks to the newly invented telegraph, word of his death circumnavigated the world. More than a hundred thousand people attended his funeral in London. "Remember," Spurgeon told his secretary just before he died, "a plain stone: 'C. H. Spurgeon,' and no more." He said, "No fuss."

Of course, Charles Spurgeon didn't get a plain stone. His tomb is one of the largest in Norwood Cemetery. It stands as a testimony to a prophecy that Spurgeon uttered only a few years before his death. In the midst of the downgrade, this is what he said: "For my part, I am quite willing to be eaten by dogs for the next 50 years, but the more distant future shall vindicate me."

In 1860, the world had declared its own prophecy of Spurgeon. An article titled "Mr. Spurgeon and the American Slave Holders" said: "Southern Baptists will not hereafter when they visit London desire to commune with this prodigy of the 19th Century. We venture the prophecy that his books in the future will not crowd the shelves of our Southern book merchants. They will not. They should not."

They were wrong. The more distant future did vindicate Spurgeon. His sermons do crowd the shelves of our bookstores. Southern Baptists came to love Spurgeon. In June of 1884, the faculty at Southern Seminary in Louisville wrote him a letter encouraging him to keep pressing on amid the disunity and the conflict. In 1892, B. H Carroll, the founder of Southwestern Baptist Seminary in Texas in Fort Worth, reflected on Spurgeon's enduring legacy: "The fire has tried his work and yet it abides unconsumed."

The golden age of the church is not behind us, brothers and sisters. It's before us. I don't know about you, but my grandmother used to say, "This ain't gold beneath my feet yet. It's hardly gravel." But a day is coming when the gravel will turn to gold. And until then, the Christ-centered sermons of the notorious English abolitionist still burn, and they still cast life and light in this dark and dying world—to the praise of the one whose glories even Spurgeon could not but begin to reveal.

---

*Some of the material in this chapter has been abridged from *The Lost Sermons of C. H. Spurgeon: His Earliest Outlines and Sermons between 1851 and 1854, Volume 1* (Nashville, TN: B&H Academic, 2017).

Additional Resources from

Colossians and Philemon for Pastors
by John Kitchen

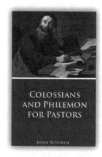

Kitchen's exposition of Colossians and Philemon is ideal for the busy pastor who loves serious Bible study. If you want to engage responsibly with biblical text, and yet get right to the point, Colossians and Philemon for Pastors will serve you well. It will guide you directly to the important questions to think through, with the added bonus of a practical ministry emphasis throughout.

—**Ray Ortlund**

God in Everyday Life: The Book of Ruth for Expositors and Biblical Counselors
by Brad Brandt and Eric Kress

How often do you run into a biblical commentary that takes you through hermeneutics, homiletics, counseling, and pastoral care—all in one volume? More than a commentary, *God in Everyday Life* is a manual on pastoral ministry. Brandt and Kress expound Ruth thoroughly, clearly, and helpfully—without taking the thrill out of it. That's a genuine compliment and a major achievement.

—**D. Ralph Davis**

The book of Ruth follows upon the dark chapters of Judges like the rising sun. And the Moabitess' radiant example shines ever bright today. How grateful I am that Rick Kress' searching expositions have been coupled with the trenchant analysis and wisdom of Brad Brandt. God in Everyday Life will grace the church both in the pulpit and personal use.   —**R. Kent Hughes**

The Discipline of Mercy (The Book of Lamentations for Pastors and Counselors)
by Eric Kress and Paul Tautges

Paul Tautges and Eric Kress have given to us a wonderful exposition of the often neglected book of Lamentations. I heartily recommend this book.

—**Walter C. Kaiser, Jr.**

Books by Bible teachers that combine solid exposition, theological depth, and pastoral wisdom are very rare. They might include one of these strengths, seldom two, but almost never all three. This book on Lamentations, however, is just such a book! It is a tremendous accomplishment. It is at one and the same time a verse-by-verse commentary, a rich devotional treasury, and a very capable guide for biblical counselors. I cannot say enough good things about it. I am grateful for this addition to the Kress Biblical Resources line of volumes. It will surely do its part to edify the church of Jesus Christ.

—**Lance Quinn**

Notes for the Study and Exposition of 1st John
by Eric Kress

I have found this treatment of 1 John very helpful in my own preparation. It is concise, well outlined, and detailed enough in the text to get at the right interpretation

—**John MacArthur**

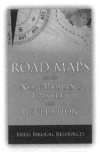

Road Maps for the Non-Pauline Epistles and Revelation
by Kress Biblical Resources

Understanding the structure of the text is key to faithful exposition. *Road Maps* lives up to its title, helping you stay on course as you study the meaning, structure, and progression of the passage. I highly commend this book as a reliable compass for biblical sermon preparation.

—**H.B. Charles Jr.**

Amillennialism and the Age to Come:
A Premillennial Critique of the Two-Age Model
by Matt Waymeyer

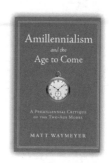

Waymeyer has written an outstanding defense of premillennialism. His work is fair, charitable, thorough, and most importantly, based on careful scriptural exegesis. Clearly there are excellent arguments on both sides of this issue, and the debate will almost certainly last until the second coming. In any case, premillennialists will be encouraged by this vigorous and scholarly defense of their reading, and amillennialists will need to interact with this impressive defense of premillennialism.

—Thomas Schreiner

Preaching Illustrations from Church History
by Ron Prosise

This is a priceless treasury of illustrative vignettes culled from church history. The anecdotes themselves make profitable, edifying reading. As sermon illustrations, they are provocative and effective. Their greatest benefit is that they will promote a deeper interest and a more thorough knowledge of church history among pastors and lay people alike. I love how Ron Prosise has catalogued and thoroughly documented this material so as to be eminently useful for preachers. This is by far the best of all the recent illustration books I have seen.

—John MacArthur

Strength in the River: Lessons in
Hope from Suffering Saints of the Bible
by Steve Swartz

The great English preacher of the nineteenth century, Charles Spurgeon, wrote, "I have learned to kiss the wave that throws me against the Rock of Ages." Can you do that when you are experiencing God's severe providence? This book will help you learn!

—John D. Street

Answering Anxiety: A Biblical Answer for What Troubles Your Heart
by Richard Caldwell

If you want biblical and God-centered help with your anxieties, I recommend enthusiastically Richard Caldwell's book ... His words are wise, encouraging, convicting, and strengthening. Take up and read!

—Thomas Schreiner

Pastor Caldwell's book on anxiety is a great example of how big things come in small packages. I recommend this book to anyone who wants to understand and address the issue of anxiety from a biblical perspective.

—Nicolas Ellen

One with a Shepherd: The Tears and Triumphs of a Ministry Marriage
by Mary Somerville (Study Guide by Mary Beeke)

I know that this book will be a source of enlightenment and encouragement to all the women who support all the men who minister to God's church.

—Elyse Fitzpatrick

I wholeheartedly recommend this book. It will help you glorify our Lord and improve and better understand your ministry marriage.

—Elizabeth George

This is a treasure of God's glory, grace, and hope for the pastor's wife. I loved reading this exceptional book and believe it will be loved by pastors' wives for many years to come.

—Martha Peace

The Upper Room
by John MacArthur

In a borrowed or rented banqueting room atop some shop or large family dwelling in Jerusalem, the drama unfolded. Jesus and His disciples were standing on the precipice of the darkest night in the history of the world. The Lord of glory was about to be betrayed and murdered. The disciples would be scattered, and the boldest of them would deny even knowing Him.

The Lord knew full well that He Himself would soon undergo an unimaginable deluge of woe. He would be spit on and mocked by evil men. He would bear the sins of the world. He would be cursed with the wrath of God for others' sins. He would feel as if His Father had utterly abandoned Him. Any other man in that situation would have been in such a state of uncontrollable agitation that He would never have been able to focus His attention on the needs of others—but Jesus was different. He wanted His followers to know the peace of the One who has overcome the world.

During those final hours before Jesus' betrayal, He gave His disciples—and consequently, all believers throughout history—His parting promises, His last will and testament. It is the inheritance of every believer in Christ.

In *The Upper Room*, Pastor John MacArthur takes us back to that night and the glorious hope we have in Christ. This is vintage MacArthur—an exposition of the text that resonates with devotion to the Lord and love for God's people, calling us to know and to love the One who loved us to the end.